American Prisoner II

-Still I Rise-

a
prisoner's personal
self-help and rehabilitation
guide

by:

D. Razor Babb and
Thomas J. Dunaway

Published by: LWL Enterprises, Inc.
P.O. Box 702862
4475 Trinity Mills Road
Dallas, TX 75370-2862

ISBN: 1-945484039
ISBN-13: 978-1-945484-03-2

Foreword

We become so absorbed in our endless striving for the world's material goals and gains that we lose sight of the riches and freedom available to us.

Our plight is similar to that of a bird that has been kept in a cage for years.

Even if the door should open, the bird is loath to fly out. Instead, it flutters from one side of the cage to another, clinging to what it knows, not wanting to venture out into the unknown.

Similarly, our souls have become so attached to our bodies that we cling to the world and worldly things and don't want to let go. True freedom does not start until we rise above body consciousness. Even when we have achieved some level of understanding, there is always more to learn and experience.

In that spirit, the higher awareness principles presented in American Prisoner I, Above the Cage, continues with the second of the series, Still I Rise. As we explore the intricacies of the of the powers beyond our 'normal' lives and get a glimpse into true freedom beyond the cage, we move onward and upward in a constant effort to better understand higher awareness.

In doing so, we refuse to allow the forces of the world to bind us, to keep us caged, or to clip our spirit's wings and to chain us to the ground; proclaiming, as we soar to a better understanding…Still I Rise.

-DRB

Note from Thomas J. Dunaway

I came to prison as a 17-year-old kid, fully invested in criminal values. I was committed to being accepted and respected and was willing to do what it took to obtain stature. Even in prison I was fully involved in criminal activity. These were my values and it showed. I did not respect rules, laws, or the rights and boundaries of others.

I was this way because I was full of hate, anger, and resentments. I was entitled and felt I had certain things coming to me. I was also filled with fear and this was a big motivator for my anger, aggression, and violence. Fear of rejection and of not fitting in, a lethal combination.

Finally, I was sent to a prison that had self-help programs and hope, and the right person took an interest in me, and spoke some truths to me that started my change and growth.

Since that time I have grown at a steady pace. My values, friends and behaviors have changed. I have educated myself in college, self-help, through self-reflection, and with the help of others, and now I live by Step-12 as much as possible. I try to be kind and understanding each and every day in all my relationships and interactions. I attempt to share the things I've been blessed enough to learn, to be a good influence, a good example, and the best version of myself that I can possibly be every day. If I can change and grow so can you, it just takes time and effort. I hope you pay forward your blessings, just as I am attempting to do. Thank you.

-Thomas J. Dunaway

AMERICAN PRISONER
II
-STILL I RISE-

TABLE OF CONTENTS

PART THREE (STILL I RISE)

Acknowledgments

Sincerest gratitude to the typewriter gods who've allowed a Frankensteined together, 18-year-old, $100 Smith-Corona to endure the labor and strain of not only AMERICA PRISONER II, but all that came before, I hope what we've produced will be of value to those who can use it most. To inhabitants of E-Pod, who so graciously allowed me to pound out these pages day after day, without complaint, thank you for your grace and assistance.

To my co-author, Thomas J. Dunaway, my appreciation for your valuable contributions to this work, I hope one day to attain even a portion of your degree of expertise in the expansive field of behavioral therapy.

And to Susan Blackburn, your above and beyond efforts during this time will be the most enduring memory of my experience of AMERICAN PRISONER II. Your love and courage are what compels me to never give up, never say die, to continuously and undauntingly not allow the pitfalls of human existence to prevent me from RISING UP even in the face of what appears to be insurmountable odds

-DRB

American Prisoner II

-Still I Rise-

PART ONE

Rise Up

CHAPTER ONE: PRISONERS OF TIME

Welcome to the second in the American Prisoner series, a prisoner's personal self-help and rehabilitation guide. Thirty-five years ago, I read a book entitled: <u>Think and Grow Rich</u>, by the esteemed self-help author Napoleon Hill. Hill devoted twenty-five years of his life interviewing the great men of his day to come up with an easy to follow guide that ordinary man could follow in order to achieve success. He theorized that if some of us could achieve prosperity, then others might as well by following the example of the fortunate ones that went before him. He interviewed Henry Ford, Andrew Carnegie, J.D. Rockefeller, J.P. Morgan, great wealthy men, the Bill Gates and Warren Buffets of his time. Then he wrote a 13-step guide, <u>Think and Grow Rich</u>, that became a best-seller and did a lot to launch the self-help boom that followed.

Little did I know at that time, that I, also, would devote twenty-five years of my life to a similar purpose. As I write this I'm entering my 25th year in captivity, twenty-eight of the last thirty spent inside these walls. When I arrived in 1993 I couldn't help but wonder, how the hell did I end up with this virtual life sentence? What was going on with me that compelled me to throw everything corresponding with the free world away and put myself in this situation? From the very beginning of this sentence I embarked on a mission to not only figure out why I'd ended up here, but how I might go about righting the wrongs I'd done, and setting a course that would lead to a worthy life.

Over the past twenty-five years I've read and studied everything I could get my hands on regarding the subjects of behavioral psychology, mindfulness, cognitive therapy, self-help, philosophy, brain science, sociology, metaphysics, spirituality, mysticism, transcendentalism, meditation and all the

1

great literary classics I could find in order to come up with a hands-on, easy to access self-rehabilitation guide that anyone can utilize in order to build a better future and lead a life they can feel proud of. I've taken the absolute best of these teachings and winnowed them down to the most useful and valuable methods and presented them in the American Prisoner series.

If you spend any significant time and effort in the study of self-improvement, you begin to see some key teachings surface again and again. There's a reason for that. For example, in Napoleon Hill's works he emphasizes that 'Thoughts are things' and 'Anything the mind of man can conceive and believe, he can achieve'. The mind of man is a wondrous thing and capable of far greater things than hustling up enough ducats to cop a bottle of wine or masterminding some elaborate scheme to work less and earn more. Although, the latter concept does have its attraction, most especially if we can apply greater free time to worthy endeavors.

Over the course of my own studies I've come across some amazing things relative to these principles. Not only have I learned them, but I've experimented and applied them to my own life. For example, did you know that you can have anything you want in life? I'm sure you've heard that said before, but think about that concept for a moment - anything you want. That covers a lot of territory. Suspend disbelief for a few seconds and ask yourself, "If I could have anything I want, like rubbing a magic lamp and my wish was fulfilled, what would you ask for?"

Several years ago, when I first began this journey of self-discovery and began applying the principles, one of the things that was required was to write out a list of goals I intended to accomplish. That list hung in the cell I was in beside my bunk for 9 years, then I moved elsewhere. At the new location, I hung the list back up by the bunk for another few years, and was moved again. Along the way the list got ripped and tattered, misplaced and buried in the bric-a-brac of loose paper and property. Then one day I happened to come across it again, some fifteen years after first writing it. It was a list of ten things I intended to accomplish, and some outlandish dreams. There were things on there like, getting a book published, starting a yard paper, finding a girlfriend, making money, getting out of prison, walking again.

You see, at the time of that initial writing I was confined to my bunk. I'd recently become paraplegic after a fall during a failed escape attempt. I was pretty torn up and it was impossibly painful even to sit up for a few minutes at a time. I'd lost most all contact with the outside world and I was on my own. There's not many prison jobs that are going to pay a guy in my position, so I was left to my own to come up with something that would provide. So,

I stared writing a two-page yard paper, *The Corcoran Sun*, in hopes it would either turn into a job or maybe I'd figure out a way to parlay it into income. After awhile, it caught on and I started soliciting advertisers. They'd send me a hundred dollars or so, or ad-trade for goods and services. A little at a time, I was earning.

One of the advertisers, *Inmate Classifieds*, had read an episodic serial drama that I was including in each edition, <u>Icicle Bill</u>. They offered to post the series on their website, a chapter at a time. Twenty-six chapters later, I had a whole book. So, I went onto the next one, <u>Goodbye Natalie</u>. It was a lot of effort to come up with these episodes, so I tended to multi-task them as much as I could. An episode of a drama series in *The Corcoran Sun* would be an episode on the website, and a chapter in a book, and if at all possible, a magazine submission or contest entry. Somehow, a couple of these episodes, or chapters, won a couple of national writing awards and that minor success led me to be inspired to continue on.

Eventually, *The Corcoran Sun* went national and was being sent to prisons in all fifty states. A small independent publisher happened to see the episodic series on-line and offered to publish the first two books for me. Along the way I started meeting people across the country and all over the world, writing from that little cell at Corcoran, and am still in contact with many of these folks to this day. And, as the years went by, I started feeling physically better. I was so engrossed with the writing and corresponding that time flew by without me noticing. When I came across that list years later it was a stunning revelation when I discovered a lot of the things I'd written there, intended as impossible dreams, had materialized.

I was writing my 10th book, I'd fallen in and out of love 3 or 4 times, I had earned a living inside that cell, and out of nowhere they'd come up with the Elderly Parole Plan, whereby I at least have a chance at getting out. And, if I can design my own leg braces, I know I can walk again. I've regained feeling all the way down to my knees and kept in shape by exercising every day since the beginning. Just about everything on that list has come true!

I'd been so busy studying and writing and applying the principles in my day-to-day life that I hadn't even noticed. It was time to make a new list, and to ramp up the studying. I started looking for the most dynamic, highest level self-help, philosophy, mindfulness teachings out there, level-4 textbook editions. I switched the fiction novel writing to prisoner self-help, because one of the most basic principles in all these teachings is that what you give is what you get. You have to be willing to share the wealth, not just monetarily, but empirically … what I know, you should know, the benefits I'm experiencing, I want you to experience. It's not just each of us alone out here, we're all interconnected in the field of energy that everyone and everything is a part of.

That's why they say, 'You can't hurt another without hurting yourself', and likewise, 'You can't help another without helping yourself'. What I'm saying here is: THIS STUFF WORKS! And I'm not just saying it, I'm living it.

I'm not trying to insinuate that it's easy, it's not. Napoleon Hill has a very poignant passage in his writings, paraphrased here: "There is one thing in life that each of us has the potential for complete control over, yet it's the most difficult thing to master. And if you are able to control that one key element, you have discovered the key to unlock the Universe. That's thing is – your own mind."

If you can harness the power in your mind, learn to control your own thoughts and direct all the power that's available to you, you can control your own destiny and open your future to limitless possibilities.

Philosopher and sage, Paul Brunton, mentioned in his great work, Perspectives, that we are all 'Prisoners of Time'. He points out that by repeating day-to-day, over and over, our habitual outlooks, memories, compulsions, neuroses – we are captured in a seemingly endless cycle of perpetual inertia that binds us to an ego-bound prison house of time and emotion where we are enslaved to each passing moment and every form of self-imposed personal suffering. It's an ego thing. This false sense of identity that believes we are separate from everyone else, untethered from the greater consciousness … alone, an island of self-determination where we have absolute authority and control. It is this ill-conceived notion of "I" ness that traps us in our tiny cages of ignorance. We are jailors of our own making. We have constructed these cells of intolerance, bigotry, suffering and small-mindedness which disallows fresh perspective.

But, not to despair friends, there is a way out of the dark caverns where the hopeless tread on graves of dreams, and the shadows shout on the nightmare screams (Maya Angelou). There is a key to unlock not only the cell door of our bars of rage, but also to open out minds to the wonderment of the vast boundless entire cosmos.

Create anything. Know anything … from within the field of our own consciousness, within our grasp, there is a Universal consciousness where all things are possible. Depending on how well we recognize that power and begin to access it, our lives and the world we live in will be affected. It's up

4

to each of us to draw forth that which we desire, and align our energy to the frequency of that which we intent to attract.

By beginning to become aware of our higher natures, higher consciousness, we can arouse ourselves to begin viewing life with new eyes as it unfolds before us in the Eternal Present, and begin to move beyond the reach of calamity. Up until now most of us interpret events that occur in our lives as 'good or bad'. Therefore, everything that happens day-to-day seems very significant, lacking greater perspective that, in a larger sense, each event is judged by the way we interpret it. And our higher nature knows that unpleasant occurrences are necessary in order to catapult us to greater understanding. The only way we grow as beings is from lessons we learn from adversities we face. Our spiritual self knows that because we are eternal in nature, these moments pass, we grow and get past them and they dissipate into the ether of eternity.

While our ego experiences the day-to-day as catastrophic, our higher self understands these seemingly momentous events are nothing more than blips on the screen that actually enhance our growth.

This doesn't mean we ignore or don't deal with the day-to-day issues, but rather we handle them in an equable manner. Rather than be enslaved in a prison of time and emotion, the only way to liberate ourselves is to rise above ego, recognize our higher nature and accept the endlessness of the eternal now, as well as the endlessness of our spiritual self.

And, by the way, just because a person is aware of these incredible powers that we all possess and has even applied them in their own life, it doesn't mean we don't still experience the usual pitfalls. For instance, three of the four girls I've had relationships with over the past few years have dumped me and never want to see or hear from me again; the outside publisher that I entrusted *The Corcoran Sun* with pretty much drove it into the ground and cut me out more or less completely; the pain I endure on a daily basis is a reminder that if you're gonna scale a 60-foot wall, wear gloves; and there's a good chance I may have to borrow a jar of coffee until I can get a package … next quarter. Oh, almost forgot, since Trump got elected it's a distinct possibility that the Elderly Parole Plan may go the way of the Edsel (a Henry Ford brainstorm that went over the cliff faster than Thelma and Louise).

But, now I have the capabilities and understanding of the greater principles and energies that enable me to withstand the storms that come. As I've heard it said, 'It's not a matter of avoiding the storms of life, but rather learning to dance in the rain.' Whatever comes, I know that is what I'm attracting into my own life and adversities that show up are lessons needed to be learned. As we go along herein we'll delve deeper into each principle mentioned, and more, much more. It's kind of like an iceberg, there's a whole lot more beneath the surface than the little bit that's apparent at first glance. And, if you're not aware of these things, blindly sailing through life, the perils and obstacles can sink you quicker that a Titanic Atlantic crossing.

Paul Brunton tells us that there is continuousness in an awareness of an eternal essence, and he's not talking about religion, although he is speaking of spirituality. By overcoming the smallness of "I", by becoming aware of the broader awakening of interconnectedness, we can access these higher energies and even create the kind of environment we most desire. The perfect people, circumstances and events will suddenly become attracted and delivered to you. By becoming aware of these greater powers, you can unlock the doors to the vast limitlessness of your mind and the entire Universe.

You can utilize the techniques you'll learn in these pages for a wide range of things … parole hearings, obtaining specific goals or objectives, self-improvement, material wealth, attracting relationships, improving your living environment or circumstances. In American Prisoner I, the concept of a higher awareness was a focal point, specifically tuning into the infinite field of energy from which everyone and everything emanates, to achieve success and attract what you want. I had an acquaintance who was preparing for a board hearing, Ramon, and he'd already been denied eight times over the years. He's heard about American Prisoner and asked if he could read it just prior to the hearing, which he did.

The hearing lasted the greater part of the day and things seemed to be going well for him. He's accomplished a lot, turned his life around; attending programs and participating, he gained insight and showed remorse, he had valid parole plans, the board seemed to like his presentation. Then, near the end of the hearing one of those unforeseen icebergs showed up in the form of the Associate District Attorney. The ADA informed the board that a confidential witness had surfaced, and this witness had information that implicated Ramon in a conspiracy to murder a witness in his case. The informant said that Ramon had told him that not only had he committed the crime in question, but he intended to have a witness that was testifying murdered. It occurred while Ramon was back in county jail, awaiting trial, on a highpower row.

Ramon was devastated. This was out of the blue and completely unexpected. Not only that, the board took it seriously; the whole mood of the room changed and he felt his chances at a favorable ruling had evaporated. In his despair, Ramon dropped his head and fell into a silent prayer, remembering the principles outlined in <u>American Prisoner</u> that explained how invisible forces come to your aid in times of need when you lift your awareness and tap into the expansive field of consciousness where we are all connected. He called upon these dormant forces at that time. And then it came to him.

He asked the ADA how was it that this informant had known who he was? How did he know his name? Well, ADA's are seasoned and trained attorneys and adept at thinking on their feet, the ADA responded that the informant got Ramon's name off of his wristband (that all county jail inmates wear). This incident was from some 30 years ago.

Ramon barely remembered his time back in county, but he remembered this. He told the ADA, and the board, "That's just not possible. I was booked into county under an alias and the whole time I was there, I used that alias. My real name was never known to anyone."

This sent the board members to the computers, calling up records, checking files, scrambling for dates. Sure enough, what Ramon said was true. Therefore, either the informant was lying or there was no informant. When Ramon came back into the board room after their deliberations, he got his approval. He told me that reading all that stuff about accessing higher energies in times of need, right before the hearing, had been the determining factor. That real-life case scenario means a lot to me. Someone had a direct benefit that resulted from reading something that came to him in the nick of time, at just the right moment. Synchronicity.

Some of the concepts presented here may seem fantastical, even impossible to some. But in order to achieve the greater things, there are times when we simply have to suspend disbelief and abandon those dreary doubts ingrained in old beliefs and just go for it. There's an old saying attributed to Henry Ford: "One man believes he can, the other believes he can't. Both are correct".

Which one do you want to be? You see, you are the one who sets the limits for yourself, or decides there are no limits. Whatever you decide, you're right.

Why are some people so lucky and seem to accomplish such amazing things and do so much while others are continuously stymied at every turn? Can we have a say in our destinies and learn to control unseen forces? Absolutely. You can create your life as you want it to be, and successful people either inherently, or through acquired knowledge, are aware of the principles that apply.

To conceptualize the limitlessness of your mind, imagine where does the air in the room end and the outside air begin? Similarly, where do your thoughts and imagination end and another's begin? What are the boundaries of your imagination? Were you born with your mind, or was it present before your conception? Does your consciousness die with your body?

The fact is there are no limits to your mind and consciousness, except those that we place upon ourselves. Think about the sun. Imagine your consciousness travelling across space to where the sun is physically located, 93 million miles away. Your imagination can have you there in a split second. It takes light travelling at 186,500 miles a second, a total of nearly 7 minutes to reach earth (from the sun). But your mind can have you there in an instant.

Now, go beyond the sun to the next nearest star visible to the naked eye, Alpha Centauri, in the constellation Centaurus. In your mind's eye, you can be there instantly. Imagine yourself sitting back in your first-grade classroom, visualize your teacher and your classmates. Or see yourself back in the neighborhood kicking it with your friends and hanging out with your best girl. Not only have you spanned the daunting distance of space, but now you are transcending time, as well. Essentially, time-traveling. Because it is readily easy to imagine being back in the old familiar place; you can see it, even hear sounds and voices and recall feelings experienced at those times as clearly as if it was happening this very moment. The mind and imagination are wonderful, powerful things, especially when you learn how to use them to your advantage.

Back to the question about where's the air outside and inside begin and end. There is no beginning or end, just like your imagination and your mind, they are everywhere. There's no place they are not. The only limitations to your mental powers are those you place on yourself.

Once you begin to understand this you'll begin to see that you can create your own world and destiny as you choose. You have the capability and power, it's simply a matter of believing and taking control.

You're not the only one with this power. Everyone and everything is a part of the same energy that's vibrating throughout the cosmos. We're all a part of the same energy field that began at the beginning of time. The higher the rate that you tune your vibrational frequency, the greater the receptivity you'll have in order to tune into the more productive, beneficial, faster energies.

All of this exists on an invisible plane and we don't learn of these things in normal grades K-12. You might get some of it if you attend college, or see it on NOVA. But for most of us, its brand new and seems incredible.

As you begin to open your mind to new things and absorb the principles and teachings, you soon realize there are great things in the world and beyond that hold immeasurable promise and potential.

Ask yourself this: Up to this point are the results you've experienced all that you really want out of life? Are you satisfied? If not, when would be the time to begin changing things, if that were possible? How about right now?

"All power is from within and therefore under our control."

-Robert Collier

Take control of your life, rise up and accept the challenge.

CHAPTER TWO: POSSIBLITY OF PAROLE

Most prisoners are doing their time with at least the notion of getting out one day, regardless of length of sentence or current circumstances. It's that hope of freedom that keeps many of us going, striving for improvement, laying the groundwork for life outside. The increasing prison population and resulting lawsuits associated with overcrowding, overwhelming taxpayer expense, and inadequate medical care have had the effect of making parole a distinct possibility for even the most hard-boiled cases. I know I did the majority of my time never thinking I'd even see a parole board. But the 2014 Elderly Parole Plan allows prisoners who have been in for at least 25 years, over the age of 60, to have a shot. There's talk of increasing that age requirement to 80, a mere 20 years more, but who's counting?

A recent *Prison Legal News* article highlights the difficulty even the most deserving prisoners face in obtaining parole. Although standards and legal definitions of eligibility criteria have been clearly defined, adherence by the parole board to these guidelines can be arbitrary and capricious. That a meth head caught with his victim's cut out heart in his pocket three days after the extraction is found suitable for parole and gets the governor's blessing, while a 70-year-old (plus) former gang shot-caller without a write-up for over 30 years gets denied, demonstrates the capricious nature of board rulings and the unfairness of the system. I know a guy in for 47 years, since he was 19, denied over and over. Even when he was found suitable one time, the governor pulled his date. Yet, he still goes to programs, still tows the line. He's got another hearing coming up next month, good luck to him. (I asked him this morning, he's been to 14 hearings!)

There are currently about 34,000 California prisoners serving life sentences with the possibility of parole. Lifers represent about 25% of the state's confined populace. There are some prisoners who have been incarcerated since the 1950's, over 60 years inside. I was housed with an 84-year-old for a time. It didn't bother him much that he was doing time, he didn't know where he was anyway.

According to UnCommon Law, the Oakland-based nonprofit organization that supports California Lifers, there are approximately 10,000 lifers in custody who have served the minimum sentence of 7, 15 or 25 years and are eligible for parole, but still remain confined. Although parole is mandated by law to release eligible prisoners when they are no longer a danger to society, and not deny parole merely based on the severity of the original crime, many prisoners are denied for arbitrary and subjective reasoning or due to petty disciplinary violations.

Most lifers face the board represented by overworked, underpaid state appointed attorneys who often perform only minimal prep work prior to the hearing. Veteran prosecutors and biased board members easily drive over many prisoners who are ill-equipped, or often, unable (mentally deficient or emotionally challenged) to present themselves in the best light.

Continued imprisonment of lifers plays a significant part in overcrowding and the burgeoning costs are supported by taxpayers. The average cost to house a prisoner is around $64,000. If just 10% of lifers currently eligible for parole were released the state would save $64 million dollars annually. Statistics show California spends $2 billion a year to house lifer inmates. This, in spite of the fact that studies show that people over the age of 40, especially those over 50, pose a very low risk of committing new crimes. The state's risk assessment stats conclude that 90% of lifers have a low to moderate risk of re-offending.

Regardless of statistics, cost and probabilities, even prisoners with extensive evidence of rehabilitative efforts and personal transformation are routinely denied. Many don't meet their state-appointed attorney prior to the hearing. These attorneys earn a max of $400 per client, which is provided to cover the costs of meeting the inmate, reviewing hundreds of pages of case files, hearing prep, travel, and hearing appearance – which may last 3 to 4 to 6 hours. Even the most dedicated attorney would find these hours and low pay daunting.

At the hearing, commissioners conduct lengthy interrogations into a prisoner's childhood and circumstances prior to the crime, the crime itself, accomplishments, rehab and discipline behind bars, and post parole plans. Prosecutors then question the prisoner, the defense attorney may pose questions as well, and all three may make closing arguments. The commissioners deliberate on spot and a decision is made.

About 20% of lifer parole hearings result in a recommendation for release. From 2011 to 2014 California Governor Jerry Brown reversed nearly 20% of grants. According to UnCommon Law, 775 lifers with murder convictions died in custody between 2000 and 2010. Many advocates say that the system is dedicated to continued incarceration, in spite of laws and policies designed to have the opposite impact.

One of the first things that occurred when Trump came into office was for Attorney General Jeff Sessions to order all federal prosecutors to seek longer sentences, and enforce existing laws to their fullest effect. This indicates the pendulum swing back towards increased warehousing of prisoners for longer terms; the 'Law and Oder' mantra of this administration erasing the Obama-era focus on rehabilitation and re-entry. It's going to get harder for us, so we have to be extra-prepared.

Presenting oneself as a model inmate at board can be, in many cases, highly difficult. Many lifers arrive to the pen in their late teens or early 20's facing the distinct possibility that they'll never go home again. Gang-involvement, constant violence or threats of violence, condition prisoners to be ready for the worst. There are drugs, alcohol, weapons, riots, peer pressure, extortion, sexual assault, intimidation (from guards as well as other prisoners). It's an atmosphere of brutality and aggression, and trying to maintain some semblance of normalcy and work toward personal enlightenment and self-rehabilitation is extremely difficult.

Even those who manage to extricate themselves from the violence and lower energy scenarios have to do so while existing in an environment where there's constant brutality, hostility, or mentally deficient prisoners at every turn. All this amid constant noise and chaos.

The gross inhumanity of prison life distorts a person's perspective and absolutely retards any self-worth that would benefit and prepare anyone for a decent life outside. There are sorrowfully few prisoners released who can honestly claim a seamless or even moderately smooth transition to outside life. You don't go from years of habitation in the depths of hell to being able to effectively deal with day-to-day issues, responsibilities and intricate interpersonal relationships, without a period of adjustment and some bumps in the road.

Reform advocates insist that meaningful programming and services for the prison populace that prioritize rehabilitative and community-based extension programs and the support of loved ones, could lead to lower recidivism and increase the likelihood of a successful transition. This could lead to lower prisoner numbers and allow the state to better invest in mental health programs and treatment and other positive, productive services.

Enlightened prison officials recognize that hope is a powerful force in personal rehabilitation. As prisoners begin to realize that they may actually go home one day, they become more engaged in programming and self-improvement. Violence and other criminal activity inside decreases when prisoners consider parole hearings as real opportunities for another chance.

WHAT TO BRING TO A PAROLE HEARING

What should you bring to a parole hearing? In light of the BPH's limit of 20 pages of material submitted on the day of the hearing, and possibly complicated by the Department of Corrections' decision not to require lifer desk staff to scan into the C-file documents submitted by inmates, it requires careful consideration. California Lifer Newsletter offers some guidelines that prisoners can follow in creating their parole packet. They say: Chronos, educational accomplishments, vocations and rules violation reports are probably already in the file available to the panel. And, the 20-page limit isn't as drastic as it seems, as the 20-page policy is a policy, not a rule, and commissioners can and do accept more than 20 pages, within reason, if they find the offered material is helpful in making their decision.

The 20-page policy is meant to prevent the panel from being presented with an excess of written material at the hearing, with the expectation that it will all be read by panel members during the deliberation portion, and remembered.

So, while the board still encourages prisoners to prepare book reports to supplement their self-help participation, don't expect the board to read entire multi-page reports done on various books. More likely, and more importantly, the panel will ask you face-to-face what you got out of a specific book and how you've been able to apply that information to your case and situation. The wiser method is to submit a summary of several books that you've read, and tell how they have helped you, while being prepared to discuss them in regard to personal impact with the commissioners at the hearing. They like to hear this directly from you.

Another important factor is that if your next hearing is a subsequent appearance, the panel will be concentrating on what you've done since your last hearing, so you don't have to go back to square one and list all of your accomplishments. And, support letters do not count toward the 20-page limit, you may have as many support letters as you can generate, and job offers, although job offers are not required to be found suitable.

The 20 pages may be double-sided (giving you 40 pages to work with). Other documents you might consider including are apology/remorse letters, workshop certificates, letters of acceptance from transitional housing, and an acknowledgement of your character flaws or triggers, and the tools you now have to deal with these issues. If you write a closing statement for the board you are free to submit that, but the panel will accept your oral presentation without a written copy.

Parole and relapse prevention plans are essential. A list of AA/NA meeting in the area where you plan to parole lets the parole board know you've thought ahead enough to locate support networks.

While you don't have to submit all your chronos, certificates and accomplishments, as the panel should have them in the C-file, it's good to have them on hand in case something isn't in the file, this way you can provide a backup copy. Some inmates bring pictures of family, home sites, skills and crafts - which are nice but have less impact than comprehensive and realistic parole plans and the understanding of causative factors and knowing your triggers. Keep in mind that the commissioners are more interested in hearing from you face-to-face than reading how well you write or flipping through a photo album or counting certificates.

CONFIDENTIAL INFORMATION

California Lifer Newsletter reports that the BPH is implementing a strategy that is intended to provide assistance to inmates and attorneys dealing with confidential information (at the hearing). The use of confidential information as grounds for a denial has been seen by many as contrary to the constitutional right to confront accusers in a judicial action.

Within the past year the BPH announced formation of a new unit in Sacramento that would review confidential information in C-files and present a summary to all parties; inmates, attorneys and DA's, in addition to the commissioners, before the hearing, in an attempt to give prisoners a chance to speak to those allegations. The unit has had a difficult time getting underway, miscalculating the magnitude of the task before them.

However, the BPH says those summary reports will be presented to all parties in the 10-day parole packet. Starting with hearings scheduled August 2017, each inmate and his/her attorney will receive a summary of items in the confidential file that the review unit feels are relative to possible suitability. The bigger news is that the review will only go back, in most cases, 10 years before the date of the hearing.

Confidential information more than 10 years old at the time of the current hearing is largely considered stale and irrelevant. Unless, of course, there are more current items in the C-file alleging similar issues

PRIVATE OR APPOINTED ATTORNEY AT BOARD

This is a big decision, both in terms of effectiveness and financially. For most inmates, it may come down to finances. A private attorney can be pricey, upwards from $2,500 in most cases, with no guarantee of results. There is highly competent appointed counsel out there, but, as previously mentioned, the $400 they're going to receive from the state barely qualifies as any form of payment. You might get lucky and find one that takes their responsibility to heart, but don't count on it.

No attorney, competent or incompetent, paid or appointed, can win parole for an unprepared client. Conversely, they probably can't lose it either, for a prisoner who is ready for parole. They can, however, be an asset.

The primary duty of counsel is to be sure their client's rights are recognized and met. They're there to put objections on record when they feel something has gone astray, and offer divergent, and accurate interpretations of the law and policy. But perhaps the main area where attorneys are of help is the behind-the-scenes pre-hearing work of preparing you for board.

This is where a private attorney has the edge over an appointed. They are sure to devote more time in helping a prisoner prepare themselves for the hearing. Since they are paid for their time and travel, this is expected. Be sure you have an agreement in writing before you commit to a private lawyer. As someone who has worked in a law firm, I know first-hand that billing (a client) can get out of hand, quickly.

For instance, any phone call automatically is computed at 15 minutes (a quarter-hour), and is billed as such. So, if your lawyer bills at say, $200 an hour, that's $50 dollars, even if you only speak for a minute. They've got rent on that fancy office, payments on the Palos Verdes ocean view house, and that Mercedes didn't come cheap. That's why a set, agreed upon TOTAL amount, in writing, is the only way to go for hearing representation. If you're going private, getting a reference from someone who has used them before is recommended.

If you end up deciding to go with the state-appointed, there are limitations you must be aware of, and you're taking the responsibility of being prepared into your own hands. That said, there is a chance of getting a good one. A lot of state-appointed attorneys are very experienced in the field and understand the nuances of the proceedings. Some of the things you should expect from them are as follows:

-   Meet with you at least 45 days prior to the hearing; in a confidential setting

-   Have reviewed your C-file and hearing packet prior to the meeting

-   Make sure that any potential communications problems (language, cognitive issues, hearing, etc.) have been identified and remedies applied for both meetings and hearings

-   Bring CDCR Form 1003 (to stipulate or waive the hearing or change attorneys) with them and see that it is filed, if necessary

-   Identify issues or documentation of possible concern at the hearing

-   Inform you of your rights and what to expect at the hearing

-   Respond to you and/or your family's letters or calls in a timely manner

-   Show up at the hearing and actively advocate for your rights

Remember, a state-appointed lawyer is appointed for only a limited scope of service, basically just for the hearing itself, and a brief pre-hearing consultation. There's no post-decision work involved, no multiple visits, or monopolization of time and attention. You get what you pay for, and you're paying zilch.

At your initial meeting, you must express your goals for the hearing. If you feel you're not ready, you might consider postponing. Maybe you feel that it's a certainty you won't get a date, but want to participate in the hearing to show growth and learn from the experience, let your attorney know this so he can help coach your presentation in those terms. But, never let any attorney pressure you into a stipulation if that isn't what you want to do. There's a difference between advice and pressure, one is expected, the other is unethical.

If you're aware that some issues and areas may be of concern, be sure to go over this pre-hearing, and let your counsel know how you are prepared to address these points. And while you may listen to advice, the ultimate decision is yours.

You are the one being assessed by the board and while an attorney can help, or hinder, the ultimate decision of suitability doesn't rest on the lawyer's performance, it's all on you. The board wants to hear from you, wants to know your story and see if you're insightful, remorseful, and ready to parole.

WRITE YOUR OWN STORY

Back in county jail I picked up a side case, 'Instrument to Aid in Escape'. Because the three-strikes law had just come into effect, late 1994, they were hot to prosecute anything they could for a 25-to-life payoff. But, this was just a side case to me, I didn't really take it seriously. I figured they would push the main case to trial, then just add on the little escape-instrument thing as a concurrent sentence. So, I took the escape on as a pro-per. That way I could get to the law library every day, and at least get a better tier on the pro-per row.

Things don't always go as planned.

A couple of years into the proceedings, after I'd been milking the pro-per routine for all I could, the judge announced that I'm going to trial … on the escape instrument. What? Yeah, tomorrow. I begged for a month to at least put up a defense, and luckily was granted that reprieve. So, for the next thirty days I prepped for a 25-to-life case that I was going to defend myself. And, they'd found the instrument, a hacksaw blade, in my legal folder at court, while I was carrying it. Tough case.

My neighbor had a bunch of law books, on everything from jury selection to closing argument. Somehow, I got the idea that I'd begin with closing argument, and jury decision, first. I'd write the thing out like a play, with that expected ending, and write backward from the 'Not Guilty' verdict that I was shooting for, all the way (backwards) from the first day of jury selection. Of course, along the way there were many unexpected turns and twists. Like when the court transport bus driver said that he knew I had the blade in my folder because someone had told him. And when a defense witness I'd summoned was turned by the A.D.A.

The noted defense lawyer, Gerry Spence, wrote a book entitled: How to Argue and Win Every Time. He pointed out that if the jury likes you, they don't want to convict you, they think with their hearts and not their heads. I took this to heart, mainly because if they were thinking with their heads, they'd surely hang me out to dry. I'd been caught red-handed, there was no disputing that fact.

Lucky for me, the A.D.A. decided that to cement a slam-dunk case, she'd let the witnesses enhance their version of the story by exaggerating the truth a bit. I caught these guys in so many lies that the jury was wondering by the end of it whether any of it was the truth. But, above all, I followed the script of the play I had written, and memorized it just like a play; including a heartfelt story presented during closing arguments about a boy and a pony.

In the middle of the story I looked over at the jury and noticed they were rocking in their chairs, riding along with me as the boy galloped over the meadow, wind in his hair. Everybody wants a pony.

When my A.D.A. got her chance at close, she suddenly had a story too. But her story began, "When I was in law school...." The jury shut down on her, they were crossing their arms and legs, frowning and grunting. They don't want to hear about your fancy, privileged better than me, law school. They want to hear about the pony!

Even with everything going against me, including a trio of idiots cutting their way out of Supermax the weekend before jury deliberations (my defense was – who breaks out of jail using a hacksaw blade?) the jury still came back in an hour with a "Not Guilty".

Point being, when you write out your board presentation, begin with the ending first - the approval for suitability. Work your way backwards though your closing argument, your parole plan, job offers, housing, recovery efforts, the crime itself, childhood, opening statement. Write it out like a play, ending first. Practice telling the story. Memorize it. Rehearse it like a live performance, because that's what it is. The performance of your life.

You might even come up with a short pony story to slip in there somewhere.

After all, who doesn't want a pony?

CHAPTER THREE: WHAT'S INSIDE

One of the interesting things about embarking on the journey and adventure of creating these chapters, is that you come across some interesting stories to pass along. As they come, sometimes I'll jot down a note to remind myself that readers might enjoy that little anecdote or fable, and many times all that remains of the story I heard is a faint memory of its telling a single time, and that brief one-line note. That's the case of that which follows, so it's very much paraphrased and probably missing some key ingredients. But, it still carries a message we can all relate to.

A long time ago in a land that your grandfathers may have known, there was this very poor man. Many people in this land were poor, but this man was so poor that even getting through the day was a struggle. He had a family, and the children many times would go hungry, the clothes they wore were no more than rags, they had to search the garbage dumps in order to survive. It was a terrible life, and no matter what this man tried to do in order to obtain money or a better life, it failed.

There was also a very rich man in this community. He had everything that anyone might desire ... a nice big house, servants, a beautiful wife and healthy children. He also had a garden that grew every kind of fruit and vegetable, land that extended for miles in each direction, and livestock of cattle, pigs, chickens, geese, and sheep. He had so much money that he didn't know what to do with it all, so he bought beautiful things from all over the world and decorated his house with them.

One day, out of desperation, the poor man went to see the rich man. He put on his best suit of worn threads, shoes with holes in the soles, and gloves which his fingers poked through. With hat in hand, he begged the rich man for a pittance, any little thing he might be able to give him that might ease his poverty and suffering. If he might be inclined to assist, he surely would be blessed from a higher source.

The rich man listened to the beggar's story and decided he would give the man something, since he saw that it wasn't easy to come to him with a hand out, and he sympathized because he knew the poor man had a family and nothing at all.

The poor man waited on the doorstep of the big house while the rich man went inside to get him his reward. When he came back, he was carrying the most beautiful gold inlaid, hand-painted glass jar. It shone in the sunlight, it's delicate craftsmanship the obvious work of the world's greatest artisans, it was a creation of beauty. The poor man gratefully accepted the gift, and thanked his benefactor. He trudged it home, cradling the gift, careful not to drop and break it.

When he got home he placed the treasured items on the fireplace mantle and looked upon it in wonder. It was the most beautiful thing that anyone had ever seen and everyone admired the jar. He took such pride and care in the jar that he wouldn't let anyone touch it, and he guarded it jealously, day and night. Although he remained poor for the rest of his life, at least he had a great treasure to own and boast of. His family still suffered great poverty, had nothing to eat, and in winter no fuel to cook or keep warm other than the sticks they could gather from the fields. Finally, the man died and was buried in a pauper's grave.

After his death, his old wife, now withered and nothing but skin and bones, one day took the prized jar down from the mantle, hoping she might take it into town and trade it for some food. As she did so, the lid fell off and shattered. She fell to her knees crying, for the value of the item surely must now be ruined because of the mishap. And as she crouched on her knees sobbing, the jar beside her, she happened to glance inside. There she saw it was filled with gold coins, enough gold to live a lifetime and more in opulence and wealth! Coin after coin, gold and more gold. Inside that jar, was enough to provide for herself and her family for all the rest of their days.

If only the man had looked inside, inside was everything he needed in order to live a rich life.

And that's the moral of the story, all any of us has to do is look inside, inside ourselves is everything we need in order to live a rich and rewarding life filled with all the good things we ever wanted or needed.

It's not what's on the outside, but what's on the inside that matters and will sustain you for a lifetime.

And, it turns out that the deeper you look inside, the more you're going to discover.

You know, you hear these things as you go through life, but until you really experience and absorb them, many times they're just words or proverbs. It took me until I was in my late 30's before I really began to understand the true meaning of what's inside.

In L.A. County jail, I happened to come across a guy that had such a profound impact on my life, that 23 years later I'm still talking about him.
Joe Hunt was one of those who just seemed to stand out among others. He has a super intellect, has a mind like a steel trap, and after coming into the system accused of involvement in a couple of murders, managed to find his way and turn his life into a shining example of what one can do, be and accomplish when they set their mind to it and find their way. He taught me about the law, public speaking, and most impactful – meditation.

This was someone I needed to meet along the way, and even though that meeting occurred during a stay in the most hellacious place on earth, I consider myself fortunate to have had the experience. Joe explained to me his own path, which led me to the path of personal enlightenment, and I'll share some of it with you here.

When Joe came to L.A. County he was under the spotlight because his case was the high-profile Billionaire Boys Club trials. Joe had established a group of wealthy progenies and was trading commodities and stocks and reaping huge dividends. But along the way trouble ensued when an unscrupulous investor cheated the Boy's Club out of a five-million-dollar sum and payback landed Joe and his comrades inside. Everybody started flipping on their leader and Joe took the fall for the whole deal.

Once inside facing all the trauma and life-destroying devastation, Joe began searching his soul for a deeper meaning. On the highpower rows of 1700-1750, he was placed in a cell that was barren, except for a mattress and a book. A single book had been abandoned there. It was <u>Autobiography of Yogi</u> by Paramahansa Yogananda. Having absolutely nothing else to do, Joe read the book, and it was a revelation. Inside those pages Yogananda tells of his life growing up in India, and his calling to become a Hindu Yogi. He knew from a very young age that this was what he was meant to do, and he ended up being responsible for bringing the teachings of the Far East to the Western World.

Within the teaching of Yogananda, meditation is considered the highest form of methodology in order to bring about peace of mind, interconnectedness, and enlightenment. In the book, he makes the sincere claim that we all can attain anything we want in life, attract anything we desire, simply by deep, heartfelt meditation … by focusing our intent on what it is we want and meditating on it and blocking out all other thoughts, feelings, emotions, distractions.

So, Joe is on the highpower row with nothing coming. There, you're in a single cell 24/7, maybe you get a shower now and then, maybe you might get rec time on the roof in a single-man cage an hour a week. If you can afford canteen, maybe you get it delivered occasionally. But it's you in the cell mostly, it's a good place to learn and practice meditation. Joe begins to wonder if the principles in <u>Autobiography of a Yogi</u> are universal and if someone locked up in Los Angeles can reap the same results as a life-long practitioner of metaphysics and transcendentalism on the other side of the world. He decided to give it a go, it's worth a chance and he comes up with a plan to test the theory. He decided he will ask for, and meditate on something completely out of the realm of possibility, so that if somehow it manifests there can be no doubt of its beyond worldly origin. He chooses to meditate on, and ask the Universe for … a donut.

He's locked down in Highpower, it's going on midnight, there's no chance he's going to come up with a donut. But, since Yogananda says that you can manifest anything you want by application of sincere meditation, this will be an extreme test. The meditation begins, and continues, and Joe finds himself lost in his meditative trance. It's peaceful, even soul-enriching, but no donuts in the vast expanse of the universal field.

The first watch guard has to walk the tiers during the night in order to do count. It's open bars on the front of the cell, so he usually walks leaning towards the outside wall. There's some violent cats in Highpower, killers and gang shot callers and guys down from death row for court. The overnight guard passes by Joe's cell and sees him meditating, probably doesn't think much of it and heads down the tier. He gets about, I don't recall, let's say 10 feet past, or a few cells down, stops, turns around and comes back to Joe's cell, and says … "Hey, Hunt, wanna donut?"

Now, you've got to know Joe Hunt to really comprehend the magnitude of the story. When Joe tells me this, he's deep into meditation and the practice of ethical existence, never telling a lie, doing the right thing, balancing your life by taking each step through life with noble intent … so it's completely impossible for him to tell a lie, or even stretch the truth. So, when he tells me this, it blows me away. But, imagine how he felt when it happened!

Out of nowhere, in the most despicable place in the galaxy, the Universe conspires to provide Joe with what he has set his intention upon, a donut.

This is the pivotal moment when Joe Hunt turned his life around and went all the way into the meditational practices that brought him enlightenment and purpose. And, lucky for me, I happened along at an opportune time in order to benefit from his illumination.

He gave me <u>Autobiography of a Yogi</u> and I read it over and over. I studied all the ancillary books and materials of the Self-Realization Fellowship, the organization that Yogananda established that brought the teaching to the West, and began meditating daily. At the height of my indoctrination I was meditating four or five hours a day in one sitting. It wasn't long until I was reaping results, for what I found in those trances was the most important discovery of my entire life. In that quiet zone where you first concentrate on your breathing, slow your metabolism down to a minimum, block out the outside world and your own swirling leaves of itinerant thoughts, there's something there that's so profound that you can't help but be affected. In that quiet peacefulness inside there's something so wondrous that it's inescapable not to notice, it is … your own soul. Right there inside, the connecting link to everything and everyone. Your higher nature, that opening portal of expansivity that connects to the energy field from which we all emanate. And out there, or in there, is the connectedness to all the other souls. You quickly realize that we are all interconnected, and you truly can't harm another without harming yourself, or help another without helping yourself. Not only that, but the answers to any problem or question, are right there in your higher awareness. You can pose any question, meditate on it, and the answer comes. It comes by focusing on it and clearing your mind in order to listen for the answer.

My God! I'd lived all those years, gone through so much hell trying to fix my problems or attain this or that goal, get this or that, feed my ego and fill my pockets. I hadn't had a clue to what was really real, what really mattered and how wondrous life could truly be. Here I was, in a rat-infested hellhole facing a life term, after losing my wife and kids, career and everything I'd ever had … but I'd found one thing that solved life's mysteries and could give me anything and everything I'd ever dreamed of. And it was right there all the time! Inside. All I needed to do, was look inside.

Of course, this doesn't mean that all my problems are over. Just because one finds the golden goose doesn't mean he isn't going to end up killing the thing. Even when you find the miracle, you have to be wise enough to apply it to your own life and be persistent and dedicated enough to implement the higher awareness into day to day life, consistently. Even when you know these things, a person's fallibility comes into play and he's sure to keep messing things up at least once in a while. Until he tires of falling down and decides the lessons life throws at him ought to be heeded instead of repeated.

But this one little chance encounter of meeting Joe Hunt opened the door for me, it changed me forever. In all the studying I've done since those days in Highpower, I've found that the higher teachings all contain similar practices and observations and realizations regarding the most basic of principles. 'Do unto others as you would have done to you' 'As a man thinketh, so shall he be' 'Thoughts are things' 'You attract that which you spend the most time thinking about' 'Love conquers all' ... on and on, Confucius, Buddha, Jesus, Mohammed, Gandhi, Martin Luther King Jr., Wayne Dyer, Norman Vincent Peale, Socrates, The Bhagavad Gita, The Bible, The Koran, all the great teachings and religions of the world, all the great philosophers and the highest level psychology texts all end up relaying similar messaging.

Tapping into our own higher natures, accessing the higher vibratory frequencies that are found during periods of inspiration, following moral and ethical codes that benefit mankind and express divinity within out innate natures, lead a life that encourages righteousness and virtue and become the light that we seek ... all of this is so close we can literally touch it, right here inside us all.

Now that we see that there is the potential for such great power that resides within each of us, we begin to look at the ways that we can apply that understanding toward our lives. Because we are criminals and have engaged in all sorts of criminal acts, there must be some mis-wiring or misunderstanding of the basic principles of following the law of the land that have occurred, leading us to these confines and restrictive habitats inside walls and fences designed to keep us separated from the outside society. The power is within us to change, to conform, even flourish, it's simply a matter of applying the knowledge in our day to day lives.

> "What we are today comes from our thoughts of yesterday, and our present thoughts build our life tomorrow; our life is the creation of our mind"
>
> -Buddha

> "Change the way you look at things, and the things you're looking at, will change"
>
> -Dr. Wayne Dyer

Jonathan Haidt writes in his best-selling pop psychology book, The Happiness Hypothesis, that the most important idea in modern psychology is contained in these simple principles and stated in these few words: Events in the world, and in our own lives, only affect us through our interpretations of them, so if we can control out interpretations, we can control our world.

More recently, on television and the Internet, Dr. Phil McGraw stated as one of his ten 'laws of life': "There is no reality, only perception." Self-help books and seminars sometimes consist of little more than lecturing and pestering people until they understand this idea and its implications on their lives. It can be inspiring to observe, when the moment comes when a person who has been consumed by years of resentment, pain, and anger realizes that their father (for example) didn't directly hurt them when he abandoned the family; all he did was move out of the house. His action was morally wrong, but the pain came from the person's reactions to the events, and if they can change their reaction, they can leave behind twenty years of pain and perhaps even get to know their father. The art of pop psychology (cognitive therapy) is to develop a method that guides people to that realization.

Haidt tells of a friend of his who had an especially negative frame of mind and was bemoaning life when someone suggested that a move to another city might suit her well. To which she replied, "No, I can be unhappy anywhere.'

> "The mind is its own place, and in itself can make a heaven of hell, or a hell of a heaven."
>
> -John Milton

Haidt, an associate professor of psychology at the University of Virginia, points out that there are three most effective ways of changing thought patterns: Meditation, cognitive therapy, and Prozac.

He has tried all of them and points out that the use of medication can have a great variety of side effects that make that type of solution prohibitive or unappealing. Meditation increases self-esteem, empathy, and trust, and even improves memory and costs nothing. Cognitive therapy is a more Western culture solution to the travails of life, and approaches problems in a more tool box methodology. Fix the problem by working on the issues that led to the issues.

There is the Freudian approach, that focuses on events in your childhood and declares, "The child is the father to the man." It entails digging through repressed memories and events in the childhood in order to change the person you are now in order to come up with a diagnosis and work through unresolved conflicts. For depressed patients, however, there's little evidence that this approach works. Later, advanced therapeutic techniques fine-tuned this process and began adopting the method of catching and training (retraining) thoughts and challenging them, creating cognitive therapy, one of the most effective treatments available for depression, anxiety and many other ailments.

Depressed people are caught in a feedback loop in which distorted thoughts cause negative feelings, which then distorts thinking further. You can break the cycle by changing the thoughts, write them down, name the distortions, and find alternative and more realistic ways of thinking. Over many weeks, the client's anxiety or depression abates. Cognitive therapy.

Haidt uses the metaphor of 'riding an elephant' to describe the human mind. While we sit atop the elephant and try to urge and guide it in the direction we want, and may know to be right, the elephant, or innate nature and desire, tends to go where it wants.

The Roman poet Ovid captured the situation well in 'Metamorphoses'; the heroine, Medea, is torn between her love for Jason and her duty to her father, she laments:

> I am dragged along by a strange new force. Desire and reason are pulling in different directions. I see the right way and approve of it, but follow the wrong.

Haidt explains that the division in the brain may be described as the 'gut' brain and the 'head' brain. The gut brain makes its independence known in many ways: It causes irritable bowel syndrome when it decides to flush out the intestines. It triggers anxiety in the head brain when it detects infections in the gut, leading you to act in more cautious ways that are appropriate when you are sick. And it reacts in unexpected ways to anything that affects the neurotransmitters, such as acetylcholine and serotonin. Hence, many of the initial side effects of Prozac and other selective serotonin reuptake inhibitors involve nausea and changes in bowel function. Trying to improve the workings of the head brain can directly interfere with those of the gut brain. The independence of the gut brain, combined with the autonomic nature of changes to the genitals, probably contribute to ancient Indian theories in which the abdomen contains the three lower chakras – energy centers corresponding to the colon/anus, sexual organs, and gut. The gut chakra is even said to be the source of gut feelings and intuitions. That is, ideas that appear to come from somewhere inside one's own mind. What St. Paul lamented as the battle of flesh versus spirit, he was surely referring to this.

"For what the flesh desires is opposed to the spirit, and what the spirit desires is opposed to the flesh; for those are opposed to each other, to prevent you from doing what you want."

-St Paul, Galatians 5:171

Or, as Ben Franklin said,

"If passion drives, let reason hold the reins."

Human rationality depends critically on sophisticated emotionality. It is only because our emotional brains work so well that our reasoning can work at all. Reason and emotion must work together to create intelligent behavior, but emotion (the elephant) does most of the work. As humans have evolved and developed over time, the brain grew and the neocortex came along, making reason (the rider, or elephant driver) possible. But, it also made the elephant smarter (and therefore, more independent.).

Freudian psychology offers a differing, yet related theory on the mind, and divisions thereof, when it categorizes the three parts:

Ego: The conscious, rational self.

Superego: The conscience, a sometimes too rigid commitment to the rules of society.

Id: The desire for pleasure, lots of it, sooner rather than later.

Haidt offers a metaphor when describing Freud's theory, as, to think of the mind as a horse and buggy in which the driver (the ego) struggles to frantically control a hungry, lustful, and disobedient horse (the id) , while the driver's father (the superego) sits in the back seat lecturing the driver on what he is doing wrong. For Freud, the goal of psychotherapy was to escape this pitiful state by strengthening the ego, thus giving it more control over the id and more independence from the superego.

But, as science and understanding evolve and develop, we begin to understand that ego itself may be a huge contributory factor to personal, emotional, cognitive maladjustments.

Why is it that we have such difficulty in carrying out our pronouncements and intentions, vows and resolutions? Why are we surprised when urges, temptations and impulses guide us to our demise? At times, we feel as though we are fighting with ourselves. It is because, we are the rider, and we are the elephant. Both have their strengths and skills, but it's a complex process to control them both. That very much begins by knowing where to look for problems that beset us; and being able to identify the issues to come up with solutions. Problems and solutions, both within the same vessel ... our own mind.

CHAPTER FOUR: THE LAW OF ATTRACTION

As I explained in the beginning of America Prisoner II, a main objective for going through all of this, writing, editing, typing, revising, mailing, copying, formatting and finally publishing, is to pass on these wonderful teachings to my fellow comrades in bondage. You don't have to spend 25 years wading through the endless volumes of self-help, psychology, spirituality and philosophy, because I've already done that and herein are the best of the best. Probably the most basic and fundamental of all principles is the law of attraction. It's actually very simple, yet the factors that are involved include quantum physics and Universal synchronicity, which are anything but simple. Yet, application can be as easy as picking up a strike three case in county. In this chapter, we'll break it down as the sooner you begin applying the fundamental principles the sooner you'll begin noticing results.

As above, so below.
As within, so without.

-The Emerald Tablet, circa 3000 BC

Rhonda Byrne wrote a self-help best seller called, The Secret, in 2006. The entire premise of the book is the law of attraction and she begins with the quote above. Can you imagine? Over five-thousand years ago people knew about and practiced the law of attraction, yet five-thousand years later we still struggle through our lives unaware of the wondrous powers available at our fingertips.

Everything that's happening with you today is the result of your own attractor patterns. You pull things, events, people to you by the frequency of the energy you radiate.

Whatever it is that you focus your mind on, that's what's coming into your life. This principle, the law of attraction, began at the very dawn of the Universe and is involved in every single spin of the planet and blink of an eyelash up to this very moment. Everything you experience in life is a result of this law, and you are responsible for calling what comes to you through your thoughts and vibratory energy.

Do you have any idea why one percent of the world's population controls 99% of the wealth? It's not an accident. That 1% understand something that the rest doesn't. They understand the law of attraction and make it work for them in order to attract wealth. They think thoughts of wealth and abundance and don't allow anything to interrupt that pattern.

Have you ever known a wealthy person who ended up losing everything? Have you noticed that within a short amount of time they were back, earning even more than before? They allowed negative thoughts to enter into their psyche and the abundance drifted away for a time, but their predominant thought pattern is that of wealth, so once they got back on track, it came back. The law of attraction responds to your thought patterns, rich or poor, whatever you focus on, that's what you get.

When you start focusing your mind on what it is you don't like, and the thoughts start spinning out of control like a swirling tornado, that's what you're going to attract – more of the stuff you don't want!

That's why it's so important to know these principles, so you can start attracting things that you do want. Your thoughts become the things you bring.

> "The predominant thought or the mental attitude is a magnet,
>   and the law of attraction reacts to the mental attitude we transmit,
>   invariably attracting such conditions as match with its nature."

> -Charles Haanel (1866-1949)

Charles Haneel was a successful businessman and author of several books. His most famous work, The Master Key System first published in 1912, provides twenty-four weekly lessons to greatness and is still read to this day.

Each of us is like a human radio or TV transmission station, sending out into the Universe messages that broadcast on a certain frequency. The frequency we transmit on, the level of our thoughts and emotions, draw back to us things, circumstances, people that are operating on a similar frequency.

To break it down further, we all know that anything and everything is made up of atoms, and sub-atomic particles, quarks and hadrons, etc.; and atoms are comprised of protons, neutrons and electrons. It's energy, electrical current, and it's spinning and gyrating and surging though every little fiber of your body, brain and even your thoughts. All of this electrical energy is flowing up your spine to your brain. If you're feeling dull and listless, the energy output is low. When you're inspired and all charged up, the frequency and output is on full. Whatever your level of energy flow, or transmission frequency, that's what you're going to attract.

That's why birds of a feather flock together. They're operating on a similar energy frequency. When you're feeling good and on a roll, you don't want to be hanging with some down and outer, they'll bring you down with them. You want to be around like-minded, similarly charged people. The high energy people are the ones emitting energy frequencies that attract all good things. The higher the frequency, the better the results.

Dr. David Hawkins, M.D., Ph.D., wrote a very clinical text on the topic of hidden determinants of human behavior, entitled, Power vs. Force. He breaks down the precise frequency measurements of forces radiated through thought patterns. At the low end, shame, guilt, apathy, grief, fear, emitting the lowest frequency vibrations, and at the high end, enlightenment, peace, joy, love, reason. On Hawkins' scale, enlightenment comes in at a whopping 700-1000 vibratory frequency, while shame has a 20. This is a scientist who is widely known as an authority within the field of consciousness research; he writes, teaches, and lectures around the world at places like Harvard and Oxford. He's applied scientific research to these principles and devoted his life to their study.

Hawkins has done clinical research involving prisoners and provides this perspective:

> "Placed in an identical and extremely stressful environment, different inmates react in ways that vary extraordinarily according to their level of consciousness. Prisoners whose consciousness is at the lowest end of the scale sometimes attempt suicide. Others become psychotic, and some become delusional. Some in the same circumstances fall into despondency, go mute, and stop eating. Still others sit with head in hands, trying to hide tears of grief. A very frequent experience is that of fear, including paranoid defensiveness.

In the same cellblock, we see other prisoners with a greater degree of energy going to rage, resulting in, violent, assaultive and homicidal behavior.

Pride is everywhere present, in the form of macho bragging and struggles for dominance.

By contrast, some inmates find the courage to face the truth of why they are there, and begin to look at their own inner lives honestly. There are always some who just 'roll with the punches' and try to get some reading done.

At the level of 'acceptance', we see prisoners who seek out help and join support groups. It is not unusual for an occasional inmate to take a new interest in learning, start studying in the prison library, or become a jailhouse lawyer (some of history's most influential political books were written behind bars). A few prisoners go through a transformation of consciousness and become loving and generous caregivers to their fellow prisoners. And it is not unheard of for a prisoner aligned with a higher energy field to become deeply spiritual, even actively pursuing enlightenment.

How we react depends on upon the world we seem to be reacting to. Who we become, as well as what we see, are both determined by perception, which can be said, simply, to create the perceptual, experiential world.

We'll examine Dr. Hawkins <u>Power vs. Force</u> further. For the moment his studies and conclusions regarding vibratory frequency is the point relative to the power of attraction, which allows scientific perspective to the concept.

A wonderful aspect regarding the law of attraction is that even if you haven't been aware of its effects on your life up to this point, once you gain insight and knowledge into its power, you can begin to change your own world in an instant. It's like awaking from a deep sleep and suddenly becoming aware of this wonderful gift, a gift of unlimited potential.

If you're creating your own life with the thoughts you have, the pictures in your mind that you see, and the level of your vibrational frequency associated with these thoughts, why not create a life of success, beauty, abundance and freedom? You may not even fully understand how it works, but most of us don't know how electricity works either, but we still use it every day.

What's important here is to begin to become aware of your thoughts and choose them carefully, because those thoughts will become what is being attracted into your life. Decide what you want to attract and start focusing on that, charge up your emotional frequency, see yourself in possession of what you want, see yourself doing what it is your desire; become obsessed and consumed with your goals and objectives and don't let anything distract you from their attainment, most of all YOURSELF! You are the number one craftsman that's creating your environment, don't waste time and energy destroying what you're working on.

The average person has about 60,000 thoughts a day. It's not reasonable to believe that we can monitor and evaluate all of these thoughts. It would be exhausting, for one thing, and probably impossible, for another. But, there's a simple indicator which we can monitor in order to get a sense of what's going on with our thought patterns – it is, how we feel.

When you're feeling good, good things seem to come. When you're on top of the world and winning, winning just keeps happening. When you're feeling bad, irritable, out of sort, dejected, down in the dumps, what's coming then? That's right, what you're attracting matches up with how you're feeling. Your feelings tell you very quickly what you're thinking. That's why you want to become aware of how you're feeling in order to take hold of yourself and get right.

There are good feelings and bad feelings. Most of the time we just run with whatever we're feeling at the time. We wake up in a bad mood or not feeling well, and the whole rest of the day is set on that course. That's how it's been. I know I've gone through most of my life being tossed to and fro that way. If I'm feeling bad then it's all bad. I don't want to hear it, I don't want to see it, it's bad to the bone, born to be bad, mad moon rising. That's where all these teachings and principles and techniques come into play. Once you begin to understand this stuff, you realize you can turn all that bad into something good. It's mind over matter, and you can take the bull by the horns and turn that gloom into a sunny room. The first thing you have to do is start feeling good.

But how do you do that when the sky is grey, your old lady just dumped you, the D.A. has decided to drop an extra charge at your doorstep, your dog died, your oatmeal is lumpy, and you just stubbed your toes getting out of bed? Having a bad day, are we? Okay, here's what you do. Since your thoughts cause your feelings, and you attract what you're thinking about, you have to learn to stop thinking about all the bad stuff going on and start thinking about something that will bring sunshine and good feelings into the mix. It's handy to have some go-to thought patterns to fall back on. I've got a few. Here are some that prove effective for me; however, you can manufacture your own, these are just examples.

I ask myself, what are the top three things that I'm grateful for? These may vary from day to day, week to week, year to year, but the top six or ten usually end up there consistently. Who or what are the things, people, circumstances that you really appreciate in your life? Think about how lucky you are for those things that you appreciate so much. Ponder on how they make you feel, start your day listing the things you're most grateful for. You might be surprised how many there are.

Next, what is your happiest memory? What has occurred in your life that no matter how many times you think about it, it brings joy? Remember that time when you felt elated, excited, inspired, wonderful? Some great victory, or happening, someone you met and fell in love with, the birth of a child, the smile of a loved one, a beautiful song that never fails to lift you up, a work of art that touches your spirit. Maybe you have a special prayer or mantra that does it for you. Whatever it is, have that in your back pocket and when you're feeling low, pull it out and open it up. Turn that bad mood into remembrance of joy, love, elation, inspiration and things will turn around for you in a good way.

Speaking of mantras, I have a few. But one of my go-to recitations is an acronym that I created for American Prisoner I. The H.A.S.L.O.V.E. list. It goes like this:

H - Honesty. Be honest with yourself and everyone else. And, am I honestly trying as hard as I can?

A – Ask and give forgiveness. To yourself and to everyone who has ever crossed you. By giving forgiveness, we unburden ourselves and live free.

S – Seek your soul. The answers to everything are right there in your heart. Your soul knows what's right, listen.

L – Live your life under control. If you're not in control, who is?

O – Own your life by giving it away. Do for others. By focusing on other people's needs, there's less emphasis on our own dilemmas.

V – Be the voice of kindness. Be kind, speak kind, do kind, think kind.

E – Exist in Eternal love. We come from a place of eternal love. Be a part of that love. Let it flood your entire being. Love is the strongest emotion, let it guide your life.

Once you begin to understand and master your own thoughts and feelings, that's when you see how you create your own reality. That's where your freedom is. That's your power.

Okay, so you are aware of this great power, how do you begin to use it? First, you state what it is that you want. Whatever it is, let the Universe know what it is. It doesn't matter what it is or how impossible it seems. Just put it out there. Next, you have to believe it. You have to know you're going to get it, it's coming, it's already ordered and you're simply waiting for delivery, it's in the mail. Next, receive it. Be open to allowing yourself to receive the great gift you're manifesting for yourself.

A very important factor here is belief. If you're telling yourself, "This may or may not work," or "This is bullshizzle," then you're already preventing yourself from attaining the goal. YOU are the one attracting, you are the one preventing! Get the heck out of your own way and allow it to happen!

Write it on a piece of paper ... "I am so happy that ..." and explain how you want your life to be or what you want. Post the paper up and look at it every day, ten times a day, a hundred! Believe and you will receive. Go ahead and obsess. It's okay if you work yourself up into a frenzy of belief and expectation, if you don't allow yourself to doubt yourself, if you believe above any and all uncertainty that you can attract what it is you are focusing on, it's going to happen.

Be clear on what it is you want, see yourself in possession of whatever it is, feel the way you'll feel when you obtain it. Napoleon Hill's famous quote says it all:

"Whatever the mind of man can conceive and believe he can achieve"

You have to believe it; therefore, it has to be a believable concept. Not only that it 'could' happen, but that it WILL happen and is happening now! Unwavering faith has a way of being rewarded. I don't know if you saw the Super Bowl where the Patriots came back from a 28-3 halftime deficit, but it was a thing of beauty and a prime example of believing. I've never seen anything like it and nothing close has ever happened in over 50 Super Bowls, but you have to believe either Brady or Belichick or Patriot's nation knew about the law of attraction.

You may have some serious medical issues you're going through that limit your physical abilities or cause you some great pain. I know something about that, and here's how I personally deal with it. When you're feeling the worst, you've got to fight back with your best. You have to tell yourself, "I feel great!" NOT good, GREAT! I feel WONDERFUL! I've never felt better! Then think about the best you've felt in your life and focus on that for a while, all the time telling yourself that you feel so good that you feel sorry for anybody that doesn't feel like you do! It's delusional, it's ridiculous, but if you want to feel better, you have to go there.

Your body is capable of some incredible things. It can heal itself by itself, imagine what it can do if you give it a little help. As strong as your body is, your mind is a hundred-thousand times stronger. If you apply your mental abilities toward the healing of your body, results will follow. If you feel a cold coming on, start meditating on 'healing cells throughout my body'. Visualize and send healing cells to the affected areas, see them rushing to heal whatever it is that's ailing you. Convince yourself that you're well and wellness follows.

Your mind is such a wondrous thing. Right there in your brain is the potential for things you're not even aware of. If you can transcend the belief system that you've been indoctrinated with all your life and begin to allow yourself to fathom that there are things and forces out there so amazing we can't conceptualize them, then you can begin to be able to tap into those unseen forces to attract things that heretofore seemed impossible.

Think about the Universe. There are billions and billions of stars out there, with planets revolving around them, and novas and supernovas and binary stars and entire galaxies that are so vast we can't imagine it. All this began somewhere, somehow, and it all interacts and even expands second to second in a cosmic dance of fluidity and synchronicity. This amazing energy field where all these galaxies co-exist in the same energy field from which we all were created and belong. So, it stands to reason, that there are forces at play we haven't considered. Because we are all a part of this great energy field, it's all the same stuff, we can tap into that expansiveness to elevate our own capabilities and do things that before now seemed impossible.

Every element that's on earth originated from the sun. We rely on solar energy to survive. This planet was once a piece of the sun, helium, hydrogen, carbon, eventually spun out into the solar system and cooled, evolving to become the life forms that are now apparent.

The sun came from that originating material that blasted out from the big bang. But what was before that? Philosophers and theologians debate this point, but most widely held beliefs consider that the originating premise most conceivable is that whatever preceded the creation of the Universe (or

Universes) is too immense to conceptualize. Many religionists label this all-creating power as God, others like to call it source energy, and that debate goes on and on. But, the one thing that I believe we can all agree upon is that there are powers out there that are far beyond our knowledge of them

These are the powers that we are tapping into to bring about these amazing circumstances into our existence. We don't have to know every detail of how the sausage is made, just how to eat it.

> "Take the first step in faith. You don't have to see the whole staircase. Just take the first step."
>
> - Dr. Martin Luther King, Jr.

Trust the Universe. Trust, believe and have faith. When I was lying in that cell in Corcoran and writing the first book, Icicle Bill, I didn't have a publisher. I didn't even know how to write a book. I just trusted that I'd do my best and whatever happened would happen as it was meant to be. It took three years to write that first book, and another three to get it published. I wrote American Prisoner in ten days and it was published in a month. The Universe provided, all we have to do is ask, believe and receive.

Think about what you want today, tomorrow, next week, next month, next year, in five, ten, fifteen years. Now set your sights and intent on that and go for it. The only thing that's stopping you is you. I've seen guys go to board hearing after board hearing, denied, denied, denied, denied… but they keep trying. They never give up. They go to programs and keep their eye on the prize, and you know what? Some of them are going to make it. I talk to O.G.'s and get a sense of their energy and intent, you get a feeling of what's going to happen. When a guy's ready, it comes. All those forces of the Universe conspire and their time comes. If we can all help those forces along, if we can attract the ones that'll give us the gifts we seek, if we know how to create our own life and destiny, then it's a waste not to utilize every force available to us, even if we don't understand it.

> "That a man can change himself … and master his own destiny is the conclusion of every mind who is wide awake to the power of right thought."
>
> Christian Larsen (1866-1954)

Expectation is a powerful attractor force. Expect the things you want and don't expect the things you don't want. Be grateful for what you already have and you will attract more good things. See yourself accomplishing your goals, and feel what it's like to succeed. The law of attraction is at work every minute of every day. Don't waste time on the negatives, or the doubts.

"Doubts are our traitors, and lead to our demise."

-Shakespeare

What are you thinking right now? What are you feeling? If it's not what you want, take charge, take control and switch to thoughts of happiness, peace, success, fulfillment, health, wealth, love, freedom. As a man thinketh, so shall he be. Be what you see, attract what you lacked. You've been given a great gift. Accept it and use it.

CHAPTER FIVE: THE LEGEND OF JHONG

A long time ago, even before the Great Wall was built in China, there was a boy that lived in a village near the Yellow River. He, his parents and his sister were poor, but they worked in the rice paddies all day together and had enough to eat and a bamboo hut, and they were happy. The boy would rush to get his work done early so he could play in the forest before it got dark. He would chase butterflies and laugh at the monkeys in the trees and skip rocks on the glittering surface of the river until his mother called him home for supper.

One evening when his mother called, he did not answer and did not come home for supper. He'd lingered in the forest too long after dark and a great tiger had found him and eaten him. The boy's soul cried out to the tiger, "Tiger, now that you have eaten me you must release my soul so I can go live with my ancestors in heaven." And the tiger responded, "Oh no, boy, you must stay with me and help me hunt, for that is the only way you may earn your freedom and go live with your ancestors in heaven."

This angered the boy, because his soul was connected to the tiger and he couldn't break free. As the tiger stalked and hunted his prey, the boy had to be there and watch. Sometimes the tiger would nap in the reeds near the river and the boy could see his parents and sister in the rice paddies, working in the sun and looking out over the land, trying to see if he was coming back to them. But he couldn't, and he couldn't tell them why. Every day he would ask the tiger, "Tiger, will you let me go so I can go live with my ancestors in heaven?" And the tiger responded, "No boy, you must remain with me and help me hunt, then I will release your soul to go to your ancestors."

As the days passed the boy did everything he could to break free from the tiger, and when the tiger hunted he would try his best to warn the prey, rustling the tree branches, yelling at the top of his lungs, throwing rocks, but all it did was create a small breeze that they barely noticed. But no matter how he begged, the tiger wouldn't release his soul, not until he agreed to help him hunt, which the boy could not do.

One day the tiger was on the far corner of the forest and there near the edge of the river lived an old wise man named Jhong. Jhong was known as a kind, generous man, and had visited the boy and his family many times, always bringing them gifts of oranges and cinnamon. The boy cried out in anguish when the tiger began stalking the old man. He knew Jhong was no match for the tiger and would surely perish. And it came to pass, the tiger caught the old man and ate him up in one big bite. The next morning the boy awoke to discover that Jhong's soul had joined him as they accompanied the tiger on his rounds. At least now he wouldn't be alone.

A few days went by and the tiger became hungry again and started stalking prey. Near the river an antelope was drinking and the tiger crept close, but every time he would get near, the antelope could hear his big feet in the grass and run away. For the next several nights the tiger would go to the river and track the antelope, but it would always hear him and run away. Finally, Jhong told the tiger, "You wait here, I'll go to the river and tell the antelope to not run away, then you can catch him and eat him." The boy heard Jhong tell this to the tiger an was angry. He was angry because the tiger had eaten him, he was angry because the tiger had eaten Jhong, and now he was even more angry because Jhong was helping the tiger catch the antelope.

After the tiger caught and killed the antelope, he didn't eat it right away, he carried it across the forest with him and they travelled all night. The boy was still angry with Jhong and asked him why he had helped the ferocious beast when it had not only killed them both, but was holding their souls captive and not allowing them to go live with their ancestors in heaven.

Jhong told the boy, "Wait and see." Near morning the tiger finally stopped when they came upon a cave in the forest. Inside the cave there were three little tiger cubs and they ate greedily. As a reward to Jhong, he freed his soul and allowed him to join his ancestors in heaven. As Jhong's soul was leaving, the boy cried because now he would be alone again, and he was confused because Jhong had helped the tiger to kill. He asked Jhong, "What will become of me?" To which Jhong replied, "Wait and see."

Over the next months that progressed into years, the boy's soul accompanied the tiger on his hunting expeditions, but he still could not bring himself to help him kill. Then one day the tiger was hunting near the rice paddies where his parents and sister lived. They were hard at work and didn't notice the tiger in the bushes. The boy tried to call out to them, but they did not hear.

It was his worst fear come true, the tiger was stalking his family! Not only that, but since the boy had been gone his sister married a neighbor boy and they had a baby. The baby was in a basket in the rice paddy, sleeping soundly as his mother worked. The boy was terrified, what was going to happen to his family and his sister's baby? The tiger could easily kill and eat them all, and he was powerless to stop it. He prayed to his ancestors to help, he prayed to the gods of earth and heavens, he prayed to old Jhong, asking, "What will I do?" The leaves rustled and a shadow from the clouds above passed over him, and in the wind, he seemed to hear old Jhong say, "Wait and see."

As the tiger crept through the brush watching the boy's family, a great commotion erupted from the far end of the field. A thunderous pounding of the earth foretold the arrival of a great beast; from the forest trees emerged a charging, enraged, sharp-horned rhinoceros galloping across the meadow and heading directly for the rice paddy where the boy's sister was working with her baby asleep beside her. The boy gasped in horror! His sister and her baby would surely be trampled and killed, and there was nothing he could do. He desperately prayed to old Jhong, "What shall I do!" to which old Jhong's spirit from heaven seemed to answer, "Wait and see."

Suddenly, the tiger burst forth from the brush and charged the rice paddy, he was powerful and fast and his stripes shone bright in the midday sun as he crossed the ground in bounding strides. At the very last second, he leapt into the air and landed on the back of the huge, thick-skinned rhino and brought it to the ground, only inches from where the sleeping baby lay. The boy's sister shrieked in fear, she quickly grabbed up the baby and ran away.

The boy was stunned and relieved at what the tiger had done, and he asked him, "Why did you do that? Why did you save my sister and her baby?" To which the tiger replied, "This is my territory, I am responsible for everyone and everything within its boundaries. That would have been a terrible accident, the rhinoceros wasn't hunting to survive, he was out of control and would have killed for no reason. I only hunt to survive and feed my children." It was then that the boy decided he would help the tiger hunt and in doing so, his soul was released to heaven where he joined his ancestors and his spirit rested in peace. He no longer hated the tiger for eating him, and he understood better that there are forces at work greater than he might ever know.

By letting go of his hatred for the tiger, by coming to understand that there are greater forces at work for greater reasons, the boy's soul was finally freed and his spirit could rest easy, joining his ancestors and old Jhong in heaven.

This is a tale of forgiveness. And a lesson to us all, because we all harbor some misplaced anger or hatred or animosity for those who have harmed us or done us wrong. As we go through life and hang onto those feelings of resentment, they weigh us down and hinder our growth. It's only by being able to forgive that we are able to move forward with a clean slate.

Dr. Wayne Dyer, the author of several self-help and higher awareness books, noted psychologist, lecturer and sage, writes in 'The Power of Intention', "Make amends with adversaries. The act of making amends sends out a signal of respect for your enemies. By radiating this forgiving energy outward, you'll find the same kind of respectful positive energy flowing back to you. By being big enough to make amends and replace the energy of anger, bitterness, and tension with kindness - even if you still insist that you're right - you'll respect yourself much more than prior to your act of forgiveness. If you're filled with rage toward anyone, there's a huge part of you that resents the presence of this debilitating energy. Take a moment right here and now to simply face that person who stands out in your mind as someone you hurt, or directed hurt to you, and tell him or her that you'd like to make amends. You'll notice how much better you feel. That good feeling of having cleared the air is self-respect. It takes much more courage, strength of character, and inner conviction to make amends than it does to hang on to the low-energy feeling."

Dyer does PBS lectures, or, he did, he passed away last year. They still replay them from time to time, if you're serious about self-improvement, I urge you to watch them. The Power of Intention is the book that really set me on a course of personal enlightenment. It covers everything you need to rise above personal circumstance and overcome that which may be holding you back from living a rewarding and enriching life. Dyer emphasizes that forgiveness is one of the main keys in unlocking your potential. You really can't take that next step without it.

He says:

"As frequently as possible, hold thoughts of forgiveness in your mind. In muscle testing, when you hold thoughts of revenge, you'll go weak, while a thought of forgiveness keeps you strong. Revenge, anger and hatred are exceedingly low energies that keep you from matching up with the attributes of the universal force. A simple thought of forgiveness toward anyone who may have angered you in the past – without any action taken on your part – will raise you to the level of spirit and aid you in individual intentions.

You can either serve Spirit with your mind or use that same mind to divorce yourself from spirit. Married to seven faces of spiritual intention (which are: Creative, Kind, Loving, Beautiful, Expanding, Abundance and Receptivity) you connect to that power. Divorced, your self-importance, your ego, takes over."

We'll cover The Power of Intention in subsequent chapters, in greater detail.

In Carlos Castaneda's great work, 'The Fire from Within', he hears these words from his sorcerer teacher:

"Self-importance is man's greatest enemy. What weakens him is feeling offended by the deeds or misdeeds of his fellow man. Self-importance requires that one spend most of one's time and life offended by something or someone."

If you can't forgive, then you're wasting your energy and your life. You must learn how to get over your own sense of self-importance and realize, there are reasons and purposes beyond your own personal narrative that control what's occurring in your life and beyond.

In Perspectives, Paul Brunton explains:

"What a higher power has decreed must come to pass. But what a man has made for himself he can modify or unmake. The first is fate; the second is destiny. The one comes from outside our personal ego, the other from our own faults. The evolutionary will of the soul is part of the nature of things but the consequences of our own actions remain, however slightly, within our own control."

Brunton goes on to explain:

"The true self of man is hidden in a central core of stillness (the center of your being-ness, your heart, your soul), a central vacuum of silence occupying only a pinpoint in dimension. All around it there is a ring of thoughts and desires, constituting the imagined self, the ego (our self-identification). This ring is constantly fermenting with fresh thoughts, constantly changing with fresh desires, and alternately bubbling with joy or heavy grief. Whereas, the center is forever at rest, the ring around it is never restful. The center bestows peace, the ring destroys it."

And yes, I understand that Brunton seems like he is 'way out there', at times, and he is. It took me 10, 15, 20 readings of some of his work to start to really comprehend where he's coming from. And I'm still working on the more esoteric of his writings. But this is someone who knows; he's spent a lifetime devoted to higher studies of philosophy and spirituality and higher-awareness. He's traveled to the farthest reaches of the earth to learn from the most revered sages, and used his brilliant mind to separate the wheat from the chaff. He understands the true essence of a person is his core spirit, that we are truly spirits, or souls inhabiting a body for this brief time we have on earth. And he puts forth great effort and energy to learn the most precious truths of human existence.

When he describes ego and our place in the cosmic scheme of things, you have to hold onto your brainpan and try not to let it spring a leak. "An ego we have, we are; its existence is inescapable if the cosmic thought is to be activated and the human evolution in it is to develop. Why has it become, then, a source of evil, friction, suffering, and horror? The energy and instinct, the intelligence and desire which are contained in each individualized fragment of consciousness, each compounded "I," are not originally evil in themselves; but when the clinging to them becomes extreme, selfishness becomes strong. There is a failure in equilibrium and gentler virtues are squeezed out, the understanding that others have rights, the feeling of goodwill and sympathy, accommodation for the common welfare – all depart. The natural and right attention to one's needs becomes enlarged to the point of tyranny. The ego then exists only to serve itself at all costs, aggressive to, and exploitive of, all others. It must be repeated: an ego must be if there is to be a world-idea. But it has to be put, and kept, in its place (which is not hardened selfishness). It must adjust to two things: to the common welfare and to the source of its own being. Conscience tells him of the first duty, whether needed or not. Intuition tells him of the second one, whether ignored or not. For, overlooked or misconstrued, the relation between evil and man must not hide the fact that the energies and intelligence used for evil derive in the beginning from the divine in man. They are God-given but turned to the service of ungodliness. This is the tragedy, that the powers, the talents, and consciousness of man are spent so often in hatred and war when they could work harmoniously for the World-idea, that his own disharmony brings his own suffering and involves others. But each wave of development must take its course, and each ego must submit in the end. He who hardens himself with gross selfishness and rejects his gentler spiritual side becomes his own Satan, tempting himself. Through ambition or greed, through dislike or hate which is instilled in others, he must fall in the end, by the Karma he makes, into destruction by his own negative side."

And here's the kicker …. "Everyone is crucified by his own ego."

This is the point where it begins getting blurry for me, when Brunton begins describing 'World-Mind and World-Idea'. He's talking about a concept of the Universe coming into existence, and God as the World-Idea, and coming into harmonious alignment with his Source (whatever that may be or whatever anyone chooses to call it).

He does point out that all spiritual study is incomplete if it ignores the facts, truths, laws and principles of the science of cosmogony (the theory or study of the origin of the Universe).

He adds,

> "When we gaze observantly and reflectively upon an object – whether it be a microscope-revealed cell or a telescope-revealed star – it inescapably imposes upon us the comprehension that an infinite intelligence rules these wonderful cosmoses. The purposive way in which the Universe is organized betrays, if anything at all, the working of a mind which understands. To recognize that the order of the cosmos is superbly intelligent beyond human invention, mysterious beyond human understanding, and even divinely holy is not to lapse into being sentimental (or overly religionist). It is to accept the transcendence and self-sufficiency of THAT WHICH IS."

Therefore, the individual, as he sees himself, in order to transcend the minor travails of life, to overcome the pettiness which binds him to the tiger of remorse and regret, selfishness and greed, must begin to become aware of the greater purpose, reason, truth. By opening ourselves to these higher ideals, we overcome the lower energy emotional attachments such as anger, frustration and self-centeredness. By forgiving, for example, we unburden and release our higher natures to something greater and more beneficent

This is an extremely busy time in my life. For the past two and a half, three months I've been working nonstop on a string of projects including helping others get their work published. In the process of doing this I've laid a great burden and load at the doorstep of my publisher. Who, coincidentally, has recently become a focal point of others who have been soliciting her for work engagements that are far more lucrative than publishing prison books. She's a freelance consultant for the aerospace industry, and a highly sought-after commodity. Billing for this type of occupation is at the highest levels, I won't go into numbers but I'm sure you can imagine what rates the top corporate consultants might require, considering the numbers involved.

The time and energy expended in relation to these assignments is relative to those rates; her personal energy and talents and abilities are stretched to the limit to meet demands. Currently, she is engaged in three high-level consulting gigs, simultaneously… and, serving as publisher for the four or five projects I'm currently working on. She hasn't hit home base in Dallas for the past four months, and the most current assignment promises to keep her away for another half-year, potentially. A beach house on Amelia Island, down the street from John Grisham, sits idle, apparently there's no time for wondrous sunrises or leisurely beach jogs when Boeing or one of the other major aerospace megalithic corporations is depending on her to deliver on-time and under budget.

It's no wonder she must roll her eyes when I grouse about the length of time it's taking to complete some prison writing project, which earns in the tens of dollars. But, she somehow, for some reason, is still always there for me, answering the call and delivering the goods. Recently, I could tell she was over-burdened and becoming over-stressed. I lay awake at night wondering what in the world I could do to help ease the tension and alleviate some of the load which, ironically, I was the source of. After becoming engaged in the writing of American Prisoner II, and spending six, seven, eight hours a day immersed in the higher teachings of Brunton and Dyer and Confucius and Buddha and Jesus, it began to sink in.

You become so absorbed in the immensity of the teachings and fed by the nourishment of the richness of the things presented in higher awareness and enlightenment doctrines, that you feel a high, a sense of the higher vibratory frequencies that come with an elevated consciousness from exposure to these teachings. There, you find the answers and solutions to day to day problems.

When we spoke today, as we do each Sunday, I couldn't wait to tell my publisher that I had come to a great realization. That none of the work I was doing was what was important, compared to the appreciation I felt for what she was doing for me and those I'm assisting. I felt such an overwhelming need to convey to her that not only did I appreciate it on a personal level, but the gratitude came from a place deep within my being. I actually felt a welling up of my heart, from the core of my being-ness I sincerely felt a heartfelt gratitude. She has done for me what no other has ever done, come to my aid in my darkest hours, come through with timely and super-human efforts that supersede all expectations, time and time again. There are few people who can affect one's life that way. And I've somehow been blessed with one.

This communication, I believe, was one of the most fulfilling and genuine moments of my life. I think I'm actually beginning to not only fathom, but apply the teachings I've been engrossed in for so long, and it's a beautiful thing. We have the power and ability to connect with others on a profound level, if we'll just take the time to consider what they might be going through and what's important to someone other than our own selfish selves. And when you put the needs of someone else before ourselves; the rewards are far greater than those you might desire for yourself.

As Wayne Dyer says:

> "The energy that creates the world, and all worlds and Universes is within you. It works through attraction and energy. Everything that's in your world, you are creating."

He goes on to quote St. Paul:

> "God is able to provide you with every blessing in abundance."

Tune into this frequency and life becomes a beautiful, wonderful event. Every thought you have has an energy attached to it that will either strengthen or weaken you. It's obviously a good idea to eliminate those thoughts that weaken you, and tune into the ones that lift you up.

Anthony de Mello offers the following in his book, One Minute Wisdom:

> "Why is everyone so happy except me?"

> "Because they have learned to see goodness and beauty everywhere," said the Master.

> "Why don't I see goodness and beauty everywhere?"

> "Because you cannot see outside of you what you fail to see inside."

A stress-free, tranquil life is a manifestation of one's grandest destiny. There is no greater reward or riches to be found. You can have all the money or fame in the world, but unless you have peace, it will never be enough.

> "So long as we believe in our heart of hearts that our capacity is limited

and we grow anxious and unhappy, we are lacking in faith. One who truly trusts in God has no right to be anxious about anything."

-Paramahansa Yogananda

You don't have to believe in God to believe the concept that if you can trust in the all creating source of the existence of everything, that which from all others and everything emanates, and tap into that all creating energy to know everything, to feel everything, to solve any of life's problems... a wonderful peace follows. In your heart, at the point where your own soul connects with all other souls, there you will find peace and the fulfillment of every dream you have ever had or will ever have.

I believe that, and I know it to be true... never more so than today, this very moment.

CHAPTER SIX: SYNCHRONICITY AND THE POWER OF INTENTION

Have you ever had the experience where the exact right person showed up at the exact right moment, that time when it seems that fate, destiny, coincidence and Karma all aligned in just the right blend of cosmic synchronicity to provide you with what you needed when you need it most? That's no accident, it occurs as a result of a force in the Universe called 'Intent'.

The great writer and philosopher Carlos Castaneda describes this force this way:

> "In the Universe there is an immeasurable, indescribable force which Shamans call intent, and absolutely everything that exists in the entire Cosmos is attached to intent by a connecting link."

Dr. Wayne Dyer wrote an entire book about it, and devoted a whole PBS special to this phenomenon, the book and the special entitled: The Power of Intention. Dyer began his career as a psychologist, then transitioned into a pop-psychology author with such works as, Your Erroneous Zones and Pulling Your Own Strings. As he progressed in his teachings and studies, he began to discover there is more to human behavior than simply the psyche and environmental influences. In his research, reading hundreds of books in the fields of psychology, sociology, philosophy and spirituality, by both ancient and modern authors, and in interviewing scholars and independent researchers, he began to become attracted to the specific study of force known as 'Intention'. The common definition of intention is a strong purpose or aim, accompanied by a determination to produce a desired result; not allowing anything to deter one in pursuit of a driving inner desire. In this limited definition, we might think of some super high-achiever, focused on some goal and not letting anything stand in their way of attainment. Like an Olympic athlete intent on a gold medal.

But, Dyer notes that in his more than 25-year study into intent he has come to the belief that it is something different than that description. He felt a shift in his thinking from purely psychological or personal-growth orientation, to a more spiritual sense, where healing, creating miracles, manifesting, and connecting to a divine intelligence are genuine possibilities. He describes this transition in thinking, from academic to spiritual, as a natural evolution, unfolded as he made a more conscious contact with spirit.

Again, I emphasize, this isn't religion. Don't confuse religion with spirituality. Religion is a manmade doctrine, while spirituality is something far beyond that.

Carlos Castaneda further describes intent as follows:

"Intent is a force that exists in the Universe. When sorcerers (those who live of the source) beckon intent, it comes to them and sets up the path for attainment, which means that sorcerers always accomplish what they set out to do."

Think about this, an invisible field of energy that's everywhere, and if you know how to access this field, anything and everything is available to you. Once Dyer discovered this dynamic, it became an obsession with him. He spent every waking moment researching it, talking about it, writing about it. He even went into open heart surgery carrying a laminated card with Castaneda's words printed on it. He wanted to know exactly what this force is, where it's located, who gets to use it, who is denied access, and why. The result of his studies was The Power of Intention, and it's probably the most inspiring self-help, personal enlightenment book I've ever come across. I've read it literally hundreds of times and it never fails to lift me up.

Believe me, I wasn't always the positive-thinker I am today. Most of my life has been spent existing in the darker, gloomier, shadowy corners where pessimism, depression, cynicism and anger reside. It took a concentrated effort to begin to emerge from the darkness and lean toward the light. And even after 25 years of study and focused effort, it's still a work in progress. Like a devoted alcoholic I was committed to my melancholia. I suppose I found comfort in the gloom. I certainly wasn't alone. There never is a lack of company in the stadium of despair. Perhaps that's why I have such belief in the principles outlined in <u>The Power of Intention</u> and the like, because if they can save me, there's hope for all of us.

The scientist David Bohm, writing in <u>Wholeness and the Implicate Order</u> concludes that all ordering influence and information is present in an invisible domain, or higher reality, and can be called upon in times of need.

<u>The Field: The Quest for the Secret Force of the Universe</u> by Lynne McTaggart, supports the existence of higher, faster energy dimension of field of intention that can be tapped in to and used by anyone.

The field is everywhere; there's no place that it's not. It affects the mosquito and tomato plants just as readily as octopuses and brontosauruses. Which is to infer, if the latter had been aware of this power, the whole extinction issue might well have been avoided.

The very source of the Universe, is intention. Pure, unbounded energy vibrating so fast that it defies measurement or observation. As Einstein and his science compatriots discovered – there is no material particle at the source... particles do not create more particles. You can break atoms down to smaller units, subatomic particles, then break those down... but at some point, you can't break them down any further. Then what have you got? If there are no particles of matter, what is there? This is intent. Source energy.

As Brunton describes it: The World-Mind, or pure thought. When it gets to that point, it becomes indescribable with words, because no one has seen it or has first-hand knowledge of it. We have what we have ... the Universe (or, Universes), stars, planets, life, and our intellects and imagination and soul consciousness.

This omnipresent energy field is accessible to all of us, and connecting to it allows us to access anything. Knowing this, why do we waste time on the day to day concerns and worries of our puny existence? It seems a ridiculous notion that we'd miss this opportunity to know anything, have anything, be able to connect to something that provides everything. All that's required is to align ourselves with the vibrational frequency of Source. Why do humans, with superior brain functions, become disconnected from Source, while fish, bugs, plants and planets go about their routine and are automatically drawn into the field without exception?

Remember the Garden of Eden?

Eve taking that first big bite of the fruit of the tree of knowledge... free choice. The ability to think for ourselves. And who knows better than we do? We're the human race, the superior life form, master to all we see, provider of all that can be provided. Really? Two-thousand years of civilization, with another several hundred thousand getting to that point, and we still think that solving conflicts through war and killing one another is the solution. Maybe we're not quite as smart as we think we are. Ending up in prison with a life sentence certainly qualifies as an example of that. And as surely as night follows day, there's absolutely no chance that we're not going to end up screwing up this world that has provided such a glorious place to reside. Pollution, atomic warfare, over-population, deterioration of natural resources, and just plain overall apathy and ignorance will eventually do us in as viable candidates for survival. The cockroaches and microbes might make it, and I'm not referring to your annoying cellmates and relatives. No wonder we're exploring Mars and Saturn, we're going to need them.

In the meantime, before we destroy the planet, if we can access the higher frequency energies to do something positive, we better do it while there's still time.

How did we become disconnected from Source and intent anyway? There are six basic beliefs that account for the separation:

1. I am what I have.

2. I am what I do.

3. I am what others think of me.

4. I am separate from everyone

5. I am separate from all that is missing from my life.

6. I am separate from Source.

It's the ego. No matter what you do, the power of the field of intention cannot be accessed through the ego. When we believe that "I" is more important than "WE" and "ALL" we have separated ourselves from the very power that can give us everything.

The recognition of the fruit of the tree of knowledge, the awareness that "I" have free will, allows an inflated sense of selfness and over-amplification of the ego, the separateness from Source, we invariably overemphasize "I".

52

Your sense of "I" ness, your feelings of self-importance are what makes you feel special. The problem with this is that when you misidentify who you truly are by identifying yourself as a body, your achievements, your possessions, you begin to identify people who have accomplished less as inferior, and your self-important superiority causes you to be constantly offended in one way or another. This misidentification is the source of most of your problems, as well as most of the problems of humankind. Feeling 'special' leads is to our self-importance.

Have you ever noticed that when you talk to people that they seem most interested in topics and things that center around 'them'? Their main interest is any interaction, thought, subject, situation, scenario that has 'them' as the focal point. Now, turn that perception onto yourself and ask if you are the same way.

With 'self' as the focal point, we sustain the illusion that we are our bodies, a complete and separate entity from all others. This sense of separateness leads us to compete rather than cooperate with everyone else. This is a huge obstacle to the connection to the power of intention. This is the ego at work, the idea of who we are, or our own self-identity. It is only by overcoming the ego that we may begin to access to higher powers.

> "Stay tuned vibrationally to the source of all life that intended you and everyone else here, and all the power of the field of intention will cooperate in order to bring into your life everything you desire."

Not a bad trade-off, let the ego domination go, get back anything and everything you've ever wanted. Creative, kind, loving, beautiful, expansive, abundant, receptive. The seven factors that describe intention. If you focus on these elements, if you shut out all the other chatter and day to day self-imposed dominant proclivities, you can access the powers that enable you to achieve greatness.

If you doubt this, you are creating a barrier to what's possible and the unlimited potential that's readily available. If you allow your doubts to stand in the way of this immense opportunity, you are denying yourself access to limitlessness and you are denying what's obvious in every flower that grows and every rain drop that falls.

Absolutely my most favorite part of the power of intention, is synchronicity. Johann Wolfgang von Goethe wrote:

> "The moment one definitely commits oneself, then Providence

53

moves too. All sorts of things occur to help one that would never otherwise have occurred... unforeseen incidents, meetings, and material assistance, which no man could have dreamed would come his way."

The right people to help you achieve your goals and objectives show up to assist you, seemingly out of nowhere. We're all part of this same field of energy, and there's no place that this infinite intent is not, you're sharing it with everyone in your life and even others that are complete strangers. But somehow, these other people are attracted to you when you need them. That's the dynamic of everything going right, the Universe conspiring to provide. When you're in the flow, the flow keeps coming. When you break the cycle, when you start having doubts or feeling disconnected, that's when the flow stops. That's your little bit of control in the greater scheme of things, you can turn it on and off just by how you're feeling, thinking, acting, doing.

When you were out there doing crime, look what happened. It led you here. When you're doing good, when you're in tune with Source energy, that's when things go well. You want to get your girl back? You want to fatten up that trust account? You want to feel better, look better, be better and get the board to see things your way? Get into the flow of the field of intention, start aligning yourself with positive attractor patterns of Creativity, Kindness, Lovingness, Beauty, Expansiveness, Abundance, Receptivity, and things will start going your way.

The right people start showing up, the right situations begin to arise, a clear pathway to what you want becomes apparent. The Universal all-creating field cooperates with you when you are vibrating at the frequency of all the good things. When you're angry, annoyed, doubtful, suspicious, resentful, hateful, it's all bad and you're attracting more bad. Not only that, when you're in the low end of the vibrational scale you're attracting bad people, people in the same mindset. And that's not good.

You can even visualize what you want coming your way, to the point of actually seeing in your mind's eye the exact person, or type of person you want to attract into your life. Sounds weird, huh? Remember, this is a Universe of attraction and energy. You can literally pull people and circumstances to your liking, by imagining and focusing on a visualized conception in your mind.

Nothing is disallowed by the Universal mind. Whatever is not allowing us to be happy or have what (or even who) we want is our own thinking.

Mystically speaking, (beyond most human comprehension and having to do with intuition, contemplation, or meditation of a spiritual nature) we are already connected to every other person by sharing the same Source energy, and in awareness of this concept. We can draw this other person or persons to us by focusing that energy upon an intended goal. You are the co-creator of what's going on and who shows up in your life.

> "I know the right person will show up and arrive in divine order at precisely the right time."

When they arrive, don't be looking the other way, either! When a truck drives by with a big five-foot high phone number on it and you're daydreaming about a Big Mac, you're missing what's been handed to you on a silver platter!

I've been writing and publishing for a few years now, starting from nothing and having to find my way, and by utilizing what the Universe has provided. I've had situations where guys will come up to me and say, "I sure wish I could get published, I wish I knew someone who would help me." Then walk away and do nothing about it. I mean they might be in the same block with me for months or years, but they just keep wandering around, watching TV, going to yard, complaining about how they wish they knew someone who would help. I have literally told people, "What do you have? Let me see your manuscript. I can help get you published." And they go about their business like there's a block wall in front of them. I was placed in their path to assist, and they didn't see it or ignored it. And there've been other guys who I have helped and they never said, "Thank You" or didn't appreciate the time and effort. They're not in tune with the forces of the Universe, and that means what? That's right, more of the same of what they've been getting.

But, we all get what we put out there. Just as you're going to get great things when you tune into the higher awareness of the field of intention, conversely, when you're operating on the lower frequencies, that's what you're attracting.

Think about the people that have showed up in your life. Your parents, siblings, wife or partner, even friends and enemies. Do you realize that they were all attracted to you at the precise moment you needed them? They have all been actors in this great play and have affected you one way or the other for their own purpose or reason.

When I was a little kid, about 4 years old, my mother and father divorced and I went with my mother. We moved away to another state and I pretty much forgot about my life before. My sister stayed with my dad and that was that. When my mother re-married and the stepfather turned out to be an abusive psychopath, I wondered why I had to endure the next nine years of psychological and physical abuse like I had. It created a real subconscious rage in me that bubbled up later in life. Welcome to the world of abused children. I am definitely not alone. There are guys in here that have endured ten times what I did, and it's no surprise places like these are filled with adults that come from that type of environment.

But, I now know that everything happens for a reason and I realize that even my own abuse had its purpose. When I was coming through L.A. County, the most vicious and brutal environment one might imagine, more than a few times I was confronted with hardcore types that were on the prowl to find victims or prove themselves. There's some real tough guys inside, no doubt. But I had a distinct advantage. You see, if a 4-year-old kid can take a beating from a full-grown man, and withstand those types of beatings for nine years, and eventually come to the point where he isn't scared anymore, just enraged to the point of saying to himself, "I'm never going to put up with anything like that again," then a few wannabe hardcores are nothing. I mean, it's laughable. Your think some lame-ass tough guy persona even compares to what I've been through? I don't care if you can beat my ass, I ain't goin' down without gettin' my licks in, bring it on.

So, you see, even the worse things that occur in life, there is a lesson there, and a purpose and reason. Sure, it might be construed that if I hadn't gone through those years of torture, I might not have ended up here. But, then I wouldn't be writing these prisoner personal self-help and rehabilitation books and enjoying the company of such a distinguished group of individuals. Hey, everybody's got to be somewhere (now that I've been here, I'm open to a more accommodating locale). And, I'm certainly working on it. Now that I'm aware there are forces out there that can provide us with anything we want and desire, believe me, I'm working on it!

One of my most favorite quotes is something that Paul Brunton expressed in <u>Perspectives,</u> and it's something I've reiterated several times within the writings:

> "The kind of experience which man most dislikes to have is the very kind which forces him to seek out its cause, and thus begin unwittingly the search for life's meaning. The disappointments in his emotional life, the sufferings in his physical body, and the misfortunes in his personal fate ought to teach him to discriminate more carefully, to examine more deeply, and in the end to feel more sympathy with the sorrowing."

What happens to a man is important, but not quite so important as what he makes of it. Out of suffering may come transmutation of values, even the transformation of character. But these developments are only possible if the man recognizes the lessons and cooperates with the guidance provided. If not, the suffering is in vain. And, personally, I refuse to allow all those years of suffering to go to waste. Out of the ashes of abuse, a phoenix of hope and discovery and limitless possibilities shall rise. Now that I know of these wondrous powers available to any and all of us, I'm all-in to access and utilize them for the greater good. Passing them onto you is part of the process and my purpose in life; taking each step with noble intent, paying it forward.

Brunton writes:

> "The experience of life, ennobling some people by degrading others, can in the end affect our thoughts, desires and feelings only as we let them. It is for us to say whether they shall call forth our divinity or our brutality. Our attitude of mind helps to determine our experiences of the world."

Sure, I wish I had learned this earlier, but I didn't. Many of us have fallen victim to our own short-comings and failures, but we can change all that. Life can be what we want it to be, what we make of it. We can start from today, from this very moment forward and have everything we want out of this life. And it's up to us, to each of us. Every single one of us has this great potential, this limitless power available to us. We can attract the wonderful people we want, the beautiful circumstances we desire, and future we dream of. It's all possible and attainable. If you don't think it's true, you're right. Because if you can't believe it, or conceive it, it won't happen for you. But if you do believe it, if you can ignore all the negative influences that have piled up around you for all these years and dig your way out of the garbage pile of the prison system and a whole lifetime of despair and struggle, and just conceive that what you want is right there at your fingertips ... all you have to do is believe, ask, receive ... then it's all yours for the asking.

I'm working on my second million dollars right now. I gave up on the first, but I'm not giving up on the second. And by a million I mean the sandy beach where the sun comes up big and orange on the horizon, a soft warm breeze drifting in through the palm trees, and the beautiful smile of a lovely face handing me my morning coffee. I don't care what anybody says or what anybody believes or doesn't believe. That's my million, and I'm going for it.

CHAPTER SEVEN: RUNAWAY TRAIN

There's a movie with Jon Voight and Eric Roberts, Runaway Train, and Voight plays a grisly con named Manny. Roberts is his younger, less-seasoned protégé. Manny and Eric escape from a prison up in some desolate, snow-covered land. They have to submerge in human waste and crawl through the prison sewer system in order to get out. There's no habitation for miles and miles, just stark snow and ice, the only viable means of transport is the train that runs a few miles out. They make it to the tracks and manage to hop a freighter, but the engineer has a heart attack and falls dead as the train moves down the track. This leaves Manny and Eric as the only passengers on this massive locomotive, rumbling down the tracks to who knows where.

I don't recall how it occurs, maybe the engineer falls against the controls as he dies, but the train is on full speed and gaining momentum as it rolls on … before long it's out of control and deemed a runaway by those monitoring the progress from a distant location. Manny and Eric are in a car separate from the engine, and with the train speeding out of control through the snow and wind, it's impossible to get to the controls. They're just passengers on a runaway, careening toward their inevitable demise. A metaphor for their actual lives as convicts and outlaws.

Manny is the quintessential convict. The meanest, cruelest, most hardcore individual one might imagine. He's got battle scars and a grimace and attitude that warn anyone that sees him, this is one dangerous, volatile individual, on a course of devastation and destruction, a human runaway train. And Eric is along for the ride. As a youngster, he admires and idolizes Manny. He wishes he could be Manny one day, but it's obvious to see, that could never be. It takes a special kind of viciousness, and an almost other-worldly brand of hate

58

and rage to be Manny, he's one of a kind.

Now, Eric and Manny don't know the train is out of control early on, so they're hiding out in the car, biding time, waiting to see where they're headed. Eric tries to engage Manny in conversation, and asks him:

"Hey, Manny, what's you gonna do when we get to where we're going? You gonna hit a big lick and get you some money and live it up good? I bet you already got some money stashed away and you're gonna get it and buy you all sorts of stuff, huh, Manny?"

Manny just looks at him, that kind of condescending stare that tells you that he doesn't like Eric, he probably doesn't like anybody though. Eric continues,

"That's what I'm gonna do. Man, I'm gonna hit a big score and get me some girls and a big car, I'm gonna have me a time, I am!" He's all excited about the prospect and trying to get Manny to join in the enthusiasm.

But Manny's just looking at him with contempt, leaning on a wall of the train car, the windows frosted over with ice and that train rumbling down the tracks, finally he says:

"You ain't gonna do none a that! You know what you're gonna do? I'll tell ya what you're gonna do. You're gonna get a little job, the only job a convict gonna get … scrubbin' a floor or cleaning out toilets. And you're gonna hold on to that job with everything you got, and you're gonna scrub that floor and clean those toilets. Then you're gonna get up the next day and do it all over again. And when the man comes to you at the end of the day and says, 'You missed a little spot over here.' You're gonna get down on your hands and knees and you're gonna scrub that little spot, and you're gonna keep scrubbing it and you're not gonna look up, 'cause you don't wanna see the fear in the man's eyes when you bash his head into the floor. 'Cept you're not gonna do that, you're just gonna keep scrubbin' and swallow all that hate. And if you can do that, then you got what it takes to be a man."

It gets quiet then in the train car. Just the sound of the rails and the train on the tracks. Eric is stunned, he didn't expect that, not from Manny, his hero. And Eric says, "I don't think I can do that … can you do that, Manny? Can you?"

Manny is staring off into space somewhere, as if remembering something from a long time ago. And he answers in a calm, almost reflective tone, as if he's maybe disappointed or disgusted with himself. He says, "I wish I could."

Manny knows that in order to conform to the rules of society he would have to go against his whole self-identification, which he knows he could never do… and, furthermore, we know that Manny realizes it's not because of his strength, but due to his weakness that this can never be. It's the pivotal point of the movie, and a turning point towards some revelation of spirit for the characters.

Manny and Eric have discovered that there is another person aboard the train, a woman. She's a freight-line employee and had been hiding because she was aware of the two convicts onboard. Flush with self-realization, perhaps the first and only time in his life that Manny has had such reflection, he decides to risk, and in all probability, sacrifice his own life in order to save the others.

For any convict, for any person wrestling with the good and evil within, this movie is a must-see. The man vs. man, man vs. nature, man vs. himself dynamics, a tribute to the classic human struggles of all humankind.

How many of us have undergone similar internal battles? How many of us have had such monumental revelations? It's our recognition of the issues facing us, and the methods with which we address them, that determine what's to become of us. And unless, until we recognize and deal with the problematic concerns we all face, we too are runaway trains destined for destruction and disaster.

All the macho yard bravado, walking around with our chests puffed out like great peacocks, crowing like cockatoos and stomping our feet like angry bulls … where's that get us? Running down the track out of control and heading for the end of the line where the inevitable collision with reality leaves us numb and dumb and dead and gone with nothing but desolation and wreckage in our wake. Is that the legacy we wish to leave behind?

For some of us, perhaps we can reclaim some air of normalcy and begin to rehabilitate ourselves through prison rehab programs, self-evaluation, self-control, education, personal enlightenment, insight, remorse and all the things society requires to become a contributing member of its club. Certainly, the Board of Parole has its criteria, and subjective qualifications, and they are all too willing to pass judgment on those of us 'lucky' enough to have a chance to come before them.

For others, like Manny, societal retribution is paid, or absolution is attained through a single act of extraordinary bravery and unselfishness, the ultimate sacrifice being given to perhaps garner some bargaining leverage in the afterlife.

> Oh, my blacke Soule! Now thou are summoned
>   By sickenesse, death's herald, and champion;
>   Thou art like a pilgrim, which abroad hath done
> Treason, and durst not turne to whence hee is fled,
>   Or like a thiefe, which till death's doom be read,
>   Wisheth himselfe delivered from prison;
>   But damn'd and hal'd to execution,
>   Wisheth that still he might be imprisoned;
>   Yet grace, if thou repent, thou canst not lacke;
>   But who shall give thee that grace to beginne?
>   Oh, my thy selfe with holy mourning blacke,
>   And red with blushing, as thou art with sinne;
> Or wash thee in Christ's blood, which hath this might
>   That being red, it dyes red soules to white.

-   John Donne (1572-1631)

Manny's black soul, at the last instant, seeks the light, even if his life-force pre-ordained a fatalistic inclination, leading to inevitable culmination of his pre-destined course.

In the higher teaching of philosophy, we learn what happens within us is intimately connected with what happens outside us. Thoughts, feelings, intuition, or character makes its secret contributions towards the events in our lives, and at the point where we begin to control ourselves and our thoughts and conduct, we will begin to control our own personal welfare.

In looking at humankind en masse, we may come to believe in the doctrine of fatalism, as it applies to the wider world. We see civilizations compelled by environment to struggle to survive like animals, this due to our not being so far removed from the animal kingdom. It's only in the last 180 thousand years or so that we even began walking upright. But, here and there emerges one or two from the herd who is becoming an individual, creatively making himself into a fully functioning human being. For him each day is a new experience, each experience unique, and each tomorrow no longer inevitable or a carbon-copy of all the yesterdays. From being enslaved by animality and fatality, he is becoming free in all humanity and creativity.

Many teachings, especially Far Eastern philosophies, attach our current state-of-affairs to Karma, and impose an iron rule of acceptance to a point of fatalism. However, although the past and our own conduct inclines us toward our present state, realistically we can still grow and improve and in doing so change the course to come. This is our free will in action, if we so choose to exercise it.

A man who commits robbery with violence may say that he is fated to act violently. With each offense, he is arrested and suffers imprisonment. After this has happened several times he begins to change his course. Eventually he fears imprisonment so much so that he resists temptation and ceases to be a criminal. This change of mental attitude is an act of free will. Even if his past inclined him to the old direction, it did not compel him.

The criminal chooses not to believe. "What you sow, you shall reap," because he does not want to believe it. Inclinations from the past do not compel a man, but he unconsciously uses them as an excuse when he thinks he can do nothing else. The will is expressed in the mental attitude a man adopts towards the situations faced. Whenever we accept the ordinary, materialistic, negative, egotistic view of a situation, we are choosing that view. Until we change our thought patterns, our behavior continues to reflect our thoughts, even if we are in denial.

Without contemplation, without recourse, our lives can become out of control like a runaway train.

CHAPTER EIGHT: POWER VS. FORCE

In Power vs. Force, Dr. David Hawkins concludes: "Man thinks he lives by virtue of the forces he can control, but in fact, he is governed by power from unrevealed sources, power over which he has no control. Because power is effortless, it goes unseen and unsuspected. Force is experienced through the senses; power can be recognized only through inner awareness. Man is immobilized in his present condition by his alignment with enormously powerful attractor energy patterns, which he himself unconsciously sets in motion. Moment by moment, he is suspended in this state of evolution, restrained by the energies of force, impelled by the energies of power.

The individual is thus like a cork in the sea of consciousness – he does not know where he is, where he came from, or where he is going, and does not know why. Man wanders about in an endless conundrum, asking the same questions century after century, and so will he continue, failing a quantum leap in consciousness. One mark of such a sudden expansion of context and understanding is an inner experience of relief, joy, and awe. All who have had such an experience feel afterwards that the Universe has granted them a precious gift. Facts are accumulated by effort, but truth reveals itself effortlessly."

The ultimate object of the investigation in Power vs. Force, is a practical understanding of the principles(s). In this respect, the Declaration of Independence provides data for the study. If you go through the sentences of the document, the source of its power appears – it is the concept that all men are equal by the divinity of their creation, the same concept that was a source of Mahatma Gandhi's power to free his nation from oppression.

Therefore, we see that true power arises from meaning. It has to do with motive and principle. Power is always associated with that which supports the significance of life itself. It appeals to human nature, or that part of it that we call noble, in contrast to force, which appeals to that which we call crass. Power appeals to that which uplifts, dignifies, and ennobles. Force must always be justified, whereas power requires no justification. Force is partial (in and of itself), power is a whole.

When we analyze the nature of force, it becomes apparent why it must always succumb to power; in accordance with the basic laws of physics. This is due to force automatically creating counter-force, therefore its effect is limited by definition. Force is like movement, it goes from here to there, or attempts to, against opposition. Power, on the other hand, stands still ... like a standing field that does not move. Gravity, for instance, does not move against anything. Its power moves all objects within its field, but the gravity field itself does not move.

Force always moves against something, whereas power does not move against anything. Force is intrinsically incomplete and therefore has to constantly be fed energy. Power is total and complete in and of itself and requires nothing from outside itself. It makes no demands, it has no needs. Because force has an insatiable appetite, it constantly consumes. Power, in contrast, energizes, gives forth life and energy. Force takes these away. We notice that power is associated with compassion and makes us feel positive about ourselves. Force is associated with judgment and tends to make us feel badly about ourselves.

Force always creates counterforce; its effects are to polarize rather than to unify. Polarization always implies conflict rather than unification. Because force incites polarization, it inevitably produces a win-lose dichotomy; and because somebody always loses, enemies are created. Constantly faced with enemies, force requires constant defense. Defensiveness is invariably costly, whether in the marketplace, politics or international affairs.

In looking for the source power, we note that it is associated with meaning and this meaning has to do with the significance of life itself. Force is concrete, literal, and arguable. It requires proof and support. The sources of power, however, are beyond argument and are not subject to proof. The self-evident is not arguable. That health is more important than disease, that life is more important than death, that honor is preferable to dishonor, that faith and trust are preferable to doubt and cynicism, that the constructive is preferable to the destructive – are all self-evident statements not subject to proof. Ultimately, the only thing we can say about a source of power is that it just 'is'.

Every civilization is characterized by native principles. If the principles are noble, it succeeds; if they are selfish, it fails. As a term, 'principles' may seem abstract, but the consequences of principles are very concrete. Principles reside in an invisible realm within consciousness itself. We can point out examples of (the principle of) honesty in the world, honesty itself as an organizing principle central to civilization is nowhere independently existent in the external world. True power, then, emanates from consciousness itself; what we see is a visible manifestation of the invisible.

Pride, nobility of purpose, sacrifice for quality of life – all such things are considered inspirational, giving life significance. But what inspires us in the physical world are things that symbolize concepts with powerful meanings to us. Such symbols realign our motives with abstract principles. A symbol can marshal great power because of the principle that already resides within our consciousness.

Meaning is important to humans. Without it, many times we lose the will to survive. Force has transient goals, when those goals are reached, there remains the vacuum of meaninglessness. Power, conversely, motivates us endlessly. If our lives are dedicated to a purpose, especially a higher purpose, our lives have meaning.

Recently defined concepts relate the understanding of the nature of power. One is physicist David Bohm's theory that states there is both a visible and invisible Universe. Don't be overwhelmed, many things exemplify this dynamic, for example: x-rays, radio and TV waves – aren't visible either. Bohm's theory states that an invisible (enfolded) Universe runs parallel to the visible 'unfolded' Universe, which itself is merely a manifestation of that enfolded, invisible Universe.

Think of it like this: the "idea" of building the world's tallest building (back in the day) garners support and results in the (invisible) concept of the Empire State Building within the visible world. The enfolded (invisible) Universe is connected with human consciousness, as inspiration arises, in the mind of the creator. Bohn says it's like mind and matter being (similar to) opposite sides of the same coin.

It's very much like Napoleon's Hill concept and declaration that "Thoughts are things", and goes very much to the heart of being able to tap into these fields of enormous power. When Roger Bannister broke the four-minute mile barrier, for example, he had to overcome the belief that it couldn't be done. Up until that time it was thought that humans could never break this invisible wall, that it wasn't humanly possible. Once Bannister broke through, however, the entire thought pattern was disrupted and reinvented, and suddenly many runners began to break the four-minute mile barrier. This occurs every time mankind breaks an old, established pattern, like the capacity to fly, the possibility to overcome alcoholism, the chance at a new life by being granted parole. Once we see that it can be done, the 'enfolded' Universe of consciousness enjoins with the physical 'unfolded' (visible) physical Universe, and the two combined create such a powerful dynamic that the before seemingly impossible, becomes possible.

When people create great works of art, come up with heretofore impossible mathematical calculations, invent something only imagined until invented, achieve some goal that previously seemed impossible, they have accessed and utilized the 'enfolded' unseen universal powers.

When you raise your emotional frequency by existing in a state of love, empathy, compassion, and forgiveness, you are aligning yourself with the unseen powers out there, tapping into the infinite. All of the great individuals throughout time have been those who aligned themselves with the power attractors. Again, and again they have stated that the power they manifested was not of themselves or their own making. All attributed the source of power to something greater than themselves.

The ability to differentiate between high and low energy patterns is a matter of perception and discrimination that most of us learn only through painful trial and error. Failure, suffering, and even sickness result from the influence of weakening patterns. In contrast, success, happiness, and health proceed from powerful attractor patterns.

Every choice we make is of great consequence and reverberates throughout our lives and beyond. The Universe doesn't forget and we ultimately have to accept responsibility for every thought, word, and deed we beget. In that sense, we create our own heaven or hell. What you're giving out, you're getting back, or eventually will.

Everything in the Universe constantly gives off the energy pattern of a specific frequency that remains for all time and can be read by those who know how. Every work, deed, thought and intention creates a permanent record. Every thought is recorded forever and there are no secrets, nothing remains hidden. Our spirits stand naked in time for all to see. Everyone's life is, ultimately, accountable to the Universe.

Knowing that, how do we reconcile ourselves to any act, thought, deed, intention of anything contrary to that we know is right and just? Take each step through life with care and noble intent, and life will reward you with all its glory and riches.

CHAPTER NINE: ADVERSITY

"When heaven is about to confer a great responsibility on any man, it will exercise his mind with suffering, subject his sinews and bones to hard work, expose his body to hunger, put him to poverty, place obstacles in the paths of his deeds, so as to stimulate his mind, harden his nature, and improve wherever he is incompetent."

- Meng Tzu, 3rd Century B.C. China

Or, as Nietszche said,

"What doesn't kill me makes me stronger."

Many traditions have a notion of fate, predestination, or divine foreknowledge. The Hindus have a belief that on the day of birth, God writes the destiny of each child on their forehead. Suppose on the day of your own child's birth, you were given the power to read this forecast, and that you could eliminate the suffering you knew was to come. What would you do? The list might include: Traumatic childhood filled with abuse and suffering. Sporadic success through adolescence, leading to a promising career in early twenties. Failed marriages and brushes with law interrupt fulfillment of potentialities during early adulthood. A prison term and severe physical maladies incur the harshest of adversities in mid-adulthood. Self-realization and spiritual enlightenment lead to personal discovery and occupational success for the last half of lifespan. What parent could resist the urge to cross off the traumas and correct the self-inflicted wounds?

But, be careful. Good intention could make matters worse. If Nietzche is right, what doesn't kill you makes you stronger, then the erasure of the severe adversity from the child's future would leave him or her weak and underdeveloped. People need adversity in order to reach the higher levels of strength, fulfillment, and personal development.

What about cases where people face the real and present threat of their own deaths, or who witness the violent deaths of others which sometimes leads to PTSD, Post-Traumatic Stress Disorder? People who suffer from PTSD are sometimes changed irreparably. A half-century of research on stress shows that it is generally bad for people and contributes to depression, anxiety disorders, and even heart disease. So, the introduction of adversity into a life can work contrary to the hypothesis of building strength and character. Therefore, it would stand to reason that it's the degree of adversity and the capacity of the individual to endure and make use of the lessons of the challenges of life that determines benefit or calamity.

POSTTRAUMATIC GROWTH

An example:

Jim's life fell apart one April evening in 2001. On that day, his wife and two children, ages four and seven, disappeared. It took Jim three days to find out that they had not died in a car crash; his wife, Jen had taken the children and run off with a man she met in a shopping mall a few weeks earlier. The four of them were driving around the country and had been spotted in several Western states. The private detective Jim hired had quickly discovered the man who had ruined Jim's life earned his living as a con man and petty criminal. How had this happened? Everything stripped from Jim's life in a single day, everything he loved most, gone. Jim visited a psychologist friend to see if he could offer insight into how his wife had fallen under the influence of such a fraud. The one insight the psychologist could offer was the man sounded like a psychopath. Most psychopaths are not violent (although serial murderers and serial rapists are psychopaths). They are mostly men, who have no moral emotions, no attachment systems, and no concern for others. Because they feel no shame, embarrassment, or guilt, they find it easy to manipulate people into giving them money, sex and trust. The psychologist told Jim that if the man was indeed a psychopath, he was incapable of love and would soon tire of Jen and the kids. Jim would probably see his children again soon.

Two months later, Jen returned. The police restored the children to Jim's custody. His panic was over, but so was his marriage, and Jim began the long and painful process of rebuilding his life. He was now a single parent living on an assistant professor's salary, and he faced years of legal expenses fighting

Jen over custody of the children. He had little hope of finishing the book that his academic career depended upon, and he worried about his children's mental health, and his own.

The psychologist friend visited Jim a few months later, and Jim told him about how the crisis had affected him. He was still in pain, but he had learned that many people cared about him and were there to help. Families from his church were bringing meals and helping with the children. His parents were selling their house in Oregon and moving nearby to help raise the kids. Also, Jim said that the experience had radically changed his perspective about what mattered in life. As long as he had his children back, career success was no longer so important to him. Jim said that he now treated people differently, a change related to his change in values. He found himself reacting to others with much greater sympathy, love, and forgiveness. He just couldn't get mad at people for little things anymore.

Jim even went the extra step to say that this was his chance to rise up and make the opportunity work for him and his children.

Two years later, he had finished his book, found a better job, and rebuilt his life. He still feels wounded by what had happened, but also realized that many positive changes had occurred due to the hardships.

For decades, research in health psychology focused on stress and the damaging effects. A major concern in this research literature has been resilience – the ways in which people cope with adversity, fend off damage, and bounce back to normal functioning. It's only recently that researchers have gone beyond resilience and began focusing on the benefits of severe stress. These benefits are referred to as 'posttraumatic growth' and in direct contrast to PTSD. People facing adversities such as cancer, heart disease, HIV, rape, assault, paralysis, infertility, house fires, plane crashes, and earthquakes have been studied, to determine how these people cope with the loss of their strongest attachments or endure such traumatic hardships. The large body of research indicates that trauma and crisis come in a thousand forms, and people benefit from them in three primary ways.

1. Rising to a challenge reveals your hidden abilities, and seeing these abilities changes your self-concept. None of us know what we're capable of enduring, until we do it. In times of severe trauma, consciousness is altered, but somehow the body keeps moving forward. One of the common factors of trauma survival is that people realize they are much stronger than they realized, and this new appreciation of their strength gives them confidence to face

future challenges.

> "Suffering produces endurance, and endurance produces character, and character produces hope."
>
> - St. Paul

> "The person who has had more experience of hardships can stand more firmly in the face of problems than the person who has never experienced suffering. From this viewpoint, some suffering can be a good life lesson."
>
> - The Dalai Lama

2. Relationships. Adversity is a litmus test. When a person is diagnosed with cancer, or a couple loses a child, or an individual goes to prison, some friends and family members rise to the occasion and look for any way they can to express support and be helpful. Others turn away, perhaps unsure of what to say or unable to overcome their own discomfort with the situation. And adversity doesn't just separate fair-weather friends from the true – it strengthens relationships and opens people's hearts to one another. We often develop love for those we care for; and we usually feel love and gratitude toward those who cared for us in a time of need.

3. Trauma changes priorities and philosophies toward the present, and changes the way we interact with others. A great many people who have faced death report changes in values and perspectives. A diagnosis of cancer is often described, in retrospect, as a wake-up call, a reality check, or a turning point. Many people consider changing careers or reducing the number of hours they spend at work. The reality that people often wake up to is that life is a gift they have been taking for granted, and that people matter more than money.

How many times do you see it in these places? Guys prioritize a few dollars above the value of a relationship with another person. An example: Recently a friend I've known for going on twenty years moved into the building. He was housed with another guy that I only recently met, an artist we'll call Vic. The first guy, we'll name, Joe, is a very worldly, likable sort. He's had a successful prison career earning good money in top jobs and investing it wisely. But Vic, although a talented and capable artist, has had mental health issues and isn't such a social success story. He gets by, utilizing his skills when and where he can. So, Joe lets Vic borrow his hot pot, which Vic (inevitably) burns to a crisp.

Now, Joe bought the hot pot for full price some years ago, probably $15-$20 and he's had it several years. Currently, and for quite a while, you can purchase a hot pot from one of the catalogs for around $8; not the same one, but a good one, I've got one myself. Joe is irate with Vic, but once he calms down he decides he can get over it, as long as Vic pays him for the loss.

I pause in the story now, and ask you, what is a fair price? The old hot pot value of $15-$20, which they don't sell anymore; or, $7-$8 for the one you can get now, which Vic could easily order through a package or Joe could put on his next package order and have Vic reimburse? Or, perhaps, some number in between?

Joe decides he is going to charge Vic, who has nothing, $24. That's the full, even inflated value of the old hot pot, at the prices last seen in catalogs, absolutely the highest dollar amount documented.

Since Vic is a bit mentally challenged, and I'm not saying he's not a brilliant guy, I'm just inferring that in interpersonal communications he doesn't always bring the best negotiating skills to the table; in cases like these he's likely to throw up his hands and declare, "Whatever!" To which Joe takes full advantage of and insists on the $24 payment.

Here's a guy that has everything he needs, and more. But money, even jailhouse money, is more important than human relationships. He doesn't care a hoot about Vic, or Vic's position, or even overall fairness. It's money over everything.

Even to the point of taking advantage of a mentally challenged guy at the first opportunity. This is a person who had been inside for some 40 years or so. An intelligent person who is seeking some sort of break from the powers that be regarding his long sentence; but has a blind-spot concerning the overall balance of the Universe, and counter-balancing wrongs done with rights that can be done.

Not only has he not learned from his own traumatic experiences, but all these years hence, is victimizing another given the opportunity.

It reminds me of Scrooge in A Christmas Carol by Charles Dickens. Scrooge, the ultimate miser, is miserable and venomous and stingy, until confronted with his own mortality in a brief meeting with the host of 'Christmases yet to come'. I still hold out hope that Joe will find that light that clicks on in time to find that generosity and compassion go a long way toward a fulfilling life.

Yet, we see by this example that not all people learn from their adversity. While many may benefit from the harsh conditions they face to grow and become a fully developed human being; others are hardened to their fellow man and rely on greed and self-serving egocentricity to warm the chilly nights.

Trauma often shatters the belief system and robs people of their sense of meaning. In doing so, it forces people to put the pieces back together again by using some higher power or purpose as a unifying principle. People sometimes seize opportunities in the ashes of a burned down life to rebuild beautifully those parts that never would have been torn down on purpose. After coping with loss or trauma some people report having grown when trying to develop a new sense of inner coherence. This coherence might not be visible to one's friends but it still feels like growth, strength, maturation, and wisdom.

> "We do not receive wisdom, we must discover it for ourselves, after
> a journey through the wilderness which no one else can make for us,
> which no one can spare us, for our wisdom is the point of view which
> we come at last to regard the world."
>
> - Marcel Proust
> -

Wisdom is the tacid knowledge that lets a person balance two sets of things. First, wise people are able to balance their own needs, the needs of others, and the needs of people or things beyond the immediate interaction. Ignorant people see everything in black and white – they rely heavily on the myth of pure evil – and they are strongly influenced by their own self-interest. The wise are able to see things from others' point of view, appreciate shades of gray, and then choose or advise a course of action that works out best for everyone in the long run. Second, wise people are able to balance three responses to their situations: adaptation (changing self to fit the environment), shaping (changing the environment), and selection (choosing to move to a new environment). The second balance corresponds roughly to the famous 'serenity prayer':

> "God, grant me the serenity to accept the things I cannot change, the
> courage to change the things I can, and the wisdom to know the
> difference."

Parents can't teach their children wisdom directly. The best they can do is to provide a range of life experiences that will help them acquire knowledge in a variety of situations. Parents can also model wisdom in their own lives and encourage children to consider situations in terms of what others might see or experience, and learn to balance their own reactions and interpretations in consideration thereof. Suffering often makes people more compassionate, helping them to find balance between self and others. Suffering often leads to active coping, reappraisal coping, or changes in plans and directions. Posttraumatic growth usually involves the growth of wisdom.

Let wisdom guide our path, learn to look for the lessons in adversity and life begins to make sense.

CHAPTER TEN: FELICITY OF VIRTUE

"It is impossible to live the pleasant life without also living sensibly, nobly and justly, and it is impossible to live sensibly, nobly and justly without living pleasantly.

-Epicurus

When wise old men and elders urge the young to seek out virtue, they aren't always received well. Some people would rather sit around the dayroom all day talking about crimes they committed or recounting the good times when they conned this one out of that, or walk around the track bitching and moaning about how terrible things are, than heed the advice of those who have gone through it or know something. Live and learn, see you next term.

I guess the Huck Finn in all of us would rather float down the Mississippi on a wooden raft, smoking a corncob pipe and fishing with a toe-line, than face up to the responsibilities that might provide some grander future, or even rewarding the present. Dorothy Gayle had to travel all the way to Oz in order to discover her divine virtues. Even the young Luke Skywalker had to leave his entire home planet behind to go out and join the galactic rebellion to discover through hard-won battles the deeper virtues and authenticity of character one uncovers through experience.

Maybe these things do have to be found out on one's own, each in their own time.

On virtue:
"Plow your fields, and you'll find what you need, you'll receive bread from your threshing floor.

Better is a bushel given you by God
Than five thousand through wrongdoing....
Better is bread with a happy heart
Than wealth with vexation"

-Amenemope

What's interesting about this quote is, it's metaphoric use of wheat and flour, ascribing the bread of life as nourishing riches earned through virtuous labor ... and, it's date of origin. This is taken from the teachings of Amenemope, an Egyptian text thought to have been written around 1300 B.C. It describes itself as an 'instruction about life' and a 'guide for well-being', promising that whoever commits its lessons to heart will discover... 'a treasure house of life to flourish on earth.' Amenemope then offers thirty chapters of advice about how to treat other people, develop self-restraint, and find success and contentment in the process.

If the quote sounds familiar to you, that's because the biblical book of Proverbs borrowed a lot from Amenemope. For example,

> "Better is a little with the fear of the Lord than great treasure and trouble with it."

-Proverbs 15:16

The entire Western civilization has been built on the foundation of virtue. The Old Testament, The New Testament, Homer, Aesop, Plato's Republic, as Western culture is largely a result of Greek philosophy, which essentially canonizes its treatises on virtues and their cultivation. And even the great thinkers realized that man's divided nature inevitably puts him at odds with himself in the battle of desire and reason.

Leave it to the Germans to come up with an alternate theory which eliminates most of the moral ambiguity, at least regarding one aspect of human persona. German philosopher Immanuel Kant believed that human beings have a dual nature: part animal and part rational. The animal part of us follows the laws of nature, just as does a falling rock or a lion killing its prey. There is no morality in nature, only cause and effect. But the rational part of us, Kant says, can follow a different kind of law – it can respect rules of conduct, and therefore can be judged morally for the degree which they respect the rules. But who then, makes the rules?

Thus, ethics and character 'rules of conduct' begin to evolve from the virtues established with the Greeks, toward a more intellectual interpretation with input from the Germans and English. If morality is about dilemmas, then moral education is training in problem solving. Children must be taught how to think about moral problems, especially how to overcome their natural egoism and take into consideration the needs of others. As such, the American ideal of ethics and virtue became, an approach that doesn't teach children what or what not to do and why, but rather, it teaches them how to think so they can decide for themselves what and what not to do, and why.

But, what of those who have none of these teachings? What of the scores of thousands and millions who find themselves raising themselves and learning by doing and fending for themselves in s complex environment such as life? The prisons in America are filled with these souls. By the time we begin figuring it out, we're on the short end of a long sentence wondering, what the hell just happened?

Not to worry my friends, we know why, don't we? The six basic virtues that make every list: wisdom, courage, humanity, justice, temperance, and transcendence (the ability to forge connections to something larger than the self) we find along the path we travel every day. The most basic: courage, wisdom and humanity ... even the cowardly lion, the scarecrow, and the tin man discovered in the end. We can only hope we are as transcendent as Dorothy when we also finally learn to put others needs before our own, and in so doing discover our way home.

That said, the following pages are designed to bring us toward a place of understanding where we may apply the principles and teachings of the previous chapters toward that worthy goal of finding the virtuous path homeward.

CHAPTER ELEVEN: INSIGHT

The following is from a brochure entitled: 'Insight' (Created by Lifers, for Lifers) and provided by the law office of Tracy Lum, 46 S. Del Puerto Ave, Suite B, #106, Patterson, California 95363.

THE IMPORTANCE OF INSIGHT

If you do not have a sufficient amount of insight, you will not be found suitable for parole. Fortunately, insight is something you can acquire and learn how to express. Insight is directly connected to responsibility and remorse. Responsibility cannot be achieved by saying you take responsibility for something and remorse cannot be shown by saying that you're remorseful. Responsibility and Remorse are shown and proved through how you express your insight into your behavior and your crime.

WHAT IS INSIGHT?

The board will want to know that you are realistic in understanding and explaining your crime. Use "I" terms and don't minimize, justify, rationalize, or blame others for the things you did and the choices you made. Insight is you being able to explain the motivation and facts of your crime. Think about how you would answer the following questions:

What led you to commit your crime?
What did you do?

How did you do it?

How did you feel about your crime at the time you were committing it?

How do you feel about your crime now?

What are the changes you have made within yourself since your arrest?

What are you doing now, as a result of the changes you have made in your life?

What will you do in the future to prevent yourself from ever committing another crime and repeating the mistakes you made?

Think about each and every question. Answer each one. Write out your answers and see if they are complete and express everything you are feeling.

Are there areas where you don't know the answers or don't understand the question? If so, seek assistance from someone you trust. You must answer them all.

WHAT DO YOU HAVE INSIGHT OF?

You must be able to explain YOUR insight into YOUR crime. The Board believes that what is written in reports in your C-file about your crime is fact. The Board will first want to see that your understanding is the same as what is written in those reports. It's best to agree with what has been written because your acceptance of the facts IS AN EXAMPLE OF HOW YOU SHOW RESPONIBILITY AND INSIGHT. If your version is not the same and you don't agree with what has been written, get proof! The Board might decide that you lack insight because you can't remember any of the facts from your crime or don't admit that what is in your reports is true. Reread all of your reports so what you say corresponds with them.

Be aware that as years go by new reports may contain incorrect information about your crime due to reinterpretation of the facts by your counselor or psychologist or even an unintentional misprint of someone else's information placed into your report (misplaced information happens more often than people realize). You will have to refer back to the original facts in order to dispute misinformation and also document your discrepancies in your one page rebuttals. Pay attention to what is written about you!

Every crime is different and it will be useful to express the factors that made your crime unique, such as:

The manner of death

The extent of the victim's injuries
The trivial reason why the crime occurred
Why you chose to avoid turning yourself in

Being able to answer these questions can be especially useful in crimes when someone was hurt or killed because it will show the Board that you understand the magnitude of what you did. If your life crime circumstances contain no loss of life or if your victim was not physically harmed, express as much insight as possible regarding who was affected in your crime and how your behavior affected or changed the lives of others.

Understanding how you were raised and how you acted before you committed your crime can also help you express insight, because it shows that you have carefully thought about negative influences of your upbringing and life prior to committing the crime

Other topics that will help you show insight are: Remorse, Causative Factors, Responsibility, Magnitude and Impact.

REMORSE

Insight into remorse means detailing WHY you are remorseful and regretful for what you did.

What are you remorseful for?
What do you specifically regret doing?

Your remorse should not only focus on what you regret doing, but also how you regret living at the time of your crime. You can discuss how you have dealt with the shame of committing your crime and injuring your victim(s) as well as express remorse by seeing the crime through the eyes of the victim(s) or the victim's family.

CAUSATIVE FACTORS

Examples of knowing the causative factors which led to a crime and why a crime occurred in the first place may include:

Bad choices
Poor criminal behavior and accepting that behavior as being O.K.
Anger, impulse, and control issues

Intoxication and drug abuse
Low self-esteem or other mental health issues
Poor associates

There are many reasons why a crime can occur. Write out and detail whatever reasons influenced and contributed to why your crime happened.

RESPONSIBILITY

What are you responsible for?

Having insight into responsibility IS responsibility, by expressing what you did wrong and what you accept responsibility for. This includes being able to accept responsibility for not only your actions, but also for your crime partners, maybe even something your victim did, or the condition you found or placed your victim in.

Taking full responsibility also means not blaming others for something you did or could have prevented. Do not compare how your crime might not be as bad as other crimes. Every victim must be given and shown the same respect as any other victim.

MAGNITUDE AND IMPACT

Life crime never has only one victim and you have to share your understanding of who and how your crime affected others. There are many victims to consider when thinking of how your crime affected others, such as:

The person(s) killed or harmed
The victim's family
The community
The witnesses
Your own family

Being able to name each of your victims, the impact of your crime, and how you changed the lives of your victims will show the Board you have thought about the immediate and long-term effects of your crime, and how it impacted those involved. Remember, if you kill someone, you take away all of their hopes and dreams, and all that they were or ever will be ... including the children that will never be due to your act(s).

WHY SHOULD WE HAVE INSIGHT?

Having insight is also evidence of growth and maturity. Grooming those qualities within yourself will help you become a better person. Without insight, you may not be able to express or show the Board that you have changed and are not the same person you were when you committed your crime.

Having remorse and taking responsibility are Board requirements. If you don't have them, you will not be considered suitable for parole. Therefore, if you don't have deep insight and a complete understanding of having remorse and taking responsibility, you won't be prepared to talk about it appropriately.

HOW DOES THE BOARD USE "INSIGHT" TO DENY PAROLE?

While you are explaining the events that led to your crime and the crime itself, the Board is listening to hear your expressions of honesty of the facts and acceptance of responsibility for what you did.

The Board will be listening to how you interpret the facts that are documented in your file and your use of terminology that might suggest you are minimizing or making excuses, manipulating, rationalizing, or trying to justify your behavior.

If the Board doesn't believe you understand what contributed to being in prison, if you don't sound like you know why you did what you did, or if you are not being realistic about what you did, they will consider that if you were released back into society, you would be a threat to the public.

WHY DOES THE BOARD USE "LACK OF INSIGHT" TO DENY PAROLE?

Many inmates actually lack insight. No one wants someone who hurts innocent people or commits crimes (and doesn't even know why they do it) to be paroled back into the community. Insight is not an exact science and because it is subjective to interpretation, the Board uses it as an opportunity to pick apart someone's presentation to create a reason to deny parole based on lack of insight.

WHAT IF WE HAVE INSIGHT AND THE BOARD STILL DENIED PAROLE?

By law, the Board should be looking for reasons to find a Lifer suitable for parole as long as that Lifer has completed all Board requirements, not search and probe for any small reason to deny someone's release. If you've done all you are supposed to do, and the Board creates or twists reasons because they just don't want to grant your parole that day, write an appeal to the court against the Board's denial decision.

You are not required to talk about the crime itself. This is a tricky issue because the Board might deny parole based on lack of responsibility by saying they couldn't understand what you were taking responsibility for. If you don't want to talk about the details of your crime (such as: due to the horrific nature of your crime), explain to the Board that you would like to utilize your right to not discuss the crime, but would like to point out that what is written in the police report, autopsy report, and probation report is true. Penal code section 5011 states that a life inmate does not have to admit guilt to the crime in order to be found suitable for parole. However, this is a very tricky area. If you have conflicting information, and are innocent of the crime, bring proof! The Board will most likely deny based on lack of taking responsibility. Appeal the decision and exhibit your proof in court.

HEARING QUESTIONS

Commissioners have asked the following questions at Board, you may be asked some of these as well. What would you say? Write out your answers.

Who were you then and who are you now? What's changed over the years?
What do you take responsibility for? When did you take responsibility? What should you have done differently?
How do you make it psychologically acceptable to deal with your crimes? Do you understand the magnitude of what you did?
What's your greatest strength? What's your greatest weakness? What do you think has changed most in you?
How'd that come about?
Where did the rage leading to the crime come from? Why did you carry

a gun?

What motivated you to commit this crime? What scenario would return you to crime?

Do you consider yourself a criminal? What do you think makes someone a criminal?

Why did you join a gang? Are you still a member? How have you broken ties?

What's your upbringing? Marriage? Children? Recent family contacts?

What effects have your actions had on others? Who have you affected?

What have you done to show remorse? When did you feel remorse?

What is the meaning of remorse? What does it mean to you?

Was your sentence fair?

What caused your crime? What causes your substance use?

What's the hardest of the 12-steps? What's step 11, 9, 8?

What are your anger triggers? What's your relapse plan?

Have you made amends to the people you have harmed? Who are the top 3?

If no amends have been made, and no opportunity presented, what would you say if given the chance? What did you put them through?

What's your disciplinary record?

What led to you turning your life around? What or who changed you the most?

What if you were confronted with the same situation today?

How can you assure the Board you'll live a life without violence?

What would you accomplish? What are your parole plans? How will you deal with stress?

Why are you suitable?

You've failed probation or parole before, what is different this time?

You'll also need a parole plan checklist, letters of support, job offers, self-help certificates, a working knowledge of 12-step programs, a relapse prevention plan, reviews of books and articles you've read and studies relating to self-rehab, educational credits, vocational training certificates, records of achievements or awards, work experience that you can rely on to obtain work. Consider writing a letter to each victim, including remorse and insight into your crimes. Additionally, housing and transitional housing acceptance and plans, 12-step program locations and times in the area you're paroling to, sponsors, where you'd go for help if needed.

You'll need a closing argument. Draft, rewrite, practice and memorize it. Make sure it covers everything in these pages. If you're ready for parole they'll know, and you'll know it.

Part II of <u>American Prisoner II, Still I Rise</u> covers specific areas of self-help, self-rehab programs that are available to those serious about self-improvement. They're presented by someone I consider to be a budding expert in these areas, Thomas J. Dunaway. I suggest reading and rereading the upcoming pages. The messages presented are valuable tools necessary to build a positive, productive future. In the hands of those who have mastered them, a life of beauty and comfort may be built.

- DRB

American Prisoner II

-Still I Rise-

PART TWO

The Change

CHAPTER TWELVE: CHANGE IS POSSIBLE

Change is possible for every one of us, even for those of us with the darkest past, change is a true option. Change is not an easy or fun process; it requires hard work, both mentally and emotionally. The work put in is a form of effort. The effort required is self-accountability. Putting in the time to read positive, healthy material that is geared towards a cognitive restructuring – changing the way you think; learning to be aware of negative thought patterns; being mindful of how you are feeling; emotional maturity, and being mindful of your behavior… all a part of change.

People say that change is hard, and it certainly is. At times, it can also be highly unpleasant. The effort required can be hard and the realization of how we have lived our lives can be unpleasant as well.

When we realize the impact we have had on other people's lives, it can make us want to quit and return to our old, familiar lifestyle patterns. Drug use, drinking, bullying, isolating, or one of the many other things we do to avoid the truth of our lives. This is one of the most challenging aspects of change, the part where we must persevere and push through. Denying or avoiding does not change the fact that we need authentic, foundational change in our lives.

The process of change can be difficult, yet the rewards of change are amazing. You will have to admit things that are difficult to admit and hard to hear; these admissions can be embarrassing, shameful, or painful. However, they are also liberating, empowering, and freeing. This difficult process can lead to an amazing life. As a result of this hard, uncomfortable process, there are great rewards.

Change is a conscious choice; a decision is made and the process begins. This is where we start to re-focus our energies on new beliefs, habits, values and social groups. Change is not an overnight, snap of the fingers event, so buckle down and prepare yourself for the new healthier choices. After the initial challenges, things will get easier and life will get better.

The first step is making the decision to change, the desire to live a healthier, more fulfilling life. We make this decision because we see the defects and problems in our lives.

There is a discrepancy in our lives that needs to be addressed, the way things are and the way we think they are, the way things are and the way we want them to be. One example is when we desire to have a good relationship with our spouse, siblings, parents or children but our beliefs and behaviors are holding us back from that, creating a discrepancy. This needs to be addressed by us, we need to change so that the nature of our relationships can change and hopefully improve. The discrepancy is our motivator, it is what helps us to realize that we have a problem and that it needs to be addressed.

Many of us doubt out ability to change. We cultivate self-defeating thoughts. We think we are not capable of change or we are not worthy, or that this life of crime and addiction is just who we are. In order to NOT think this way, we need to think a different way. Sounds simple, doesn't it? After a lot of holding ourselves accountable, it is possible.

When you first begin to try changing, you will have to remind yourself that you are worthy, that you are deserving, that you can change and that your life will be better for it. But to do so, you will have to motivate yourself time and time again, and after enough time and effort has passed, this will become less and less necessary, and you will overcome self-doubt. One thing you must be aware of is self-sabotage, putting yourself in situations where you will fail. Situations like hanging around old friends, around drugs and the drug scene, alcohol, unhealthy people or places or things. Make a list of these people, places and things, and stay away from them until you develop the coping skills to deal with them in short intervals.

Change involves goal setting. This is important and will be covered in a separate chapter.

Exposing yourself to new information and ways of living is vital when trying to shake old habits and ways of thinking. If you don't expose yourself to new things you are going to continue to think and behave in the same way old way, be around the same people, in the same places; none of which will support change.

In order to change these things, we have to recognize them. Start by making lists. What thoughts can lead you to bad choices? No one likes me, no one loves me. No one cares about me. I can't get a good job. I can just sell a little dope and get on my feet. I can steal something and come up.

What types of thoughts lead to trouble? When we live a life of addiction, whether it is to drugs or irrational ways of thinking, we need to be aware of how we think and then map it out, so we can change it; changing the way we feel and how we act or behave. This type of change requires self-honesty – being able to admit to ourselves what it is we are really thinking. Owning it, at least to yourself. As Step 5 says, admit it to God, myself, and another. Start with yourself. This is the beginning in the process of change.

Becoming "MINDFUL" of yourself is an effective tool. To be mindful means to be consciously aware of how you are thinking or feeling. This mindfulness means you need to be aware of negative or unhealthy thought patterns. The earlier on that you can gain awareness into these patterns the better.

An example would be thinking of getting high. "I'm tired of all this crap. I sure could use a shot right now. If I could just get away from this for a few hours, I'd be cool." We know we can't get "away" for a few hours. So, if we can catch this thinking early on, we can begin to counter it with some healthy thoughts, some distractions from the negative cycle. Once these thoughts begin, we play them over and over in our minds until we act on them. We have to break this cycle. The easiest way to do this is to catch it early! Do not allow it to get started and to gain traction. That thinking leads to bad choices which end up with bad consequences.

This is cognitive restructuring. This means we restructure (change) how we think. To do this we need to become aware of irrational, unhealthy thoughts, this is why mapping our thoughts is so important. When we start to have these irrational thoughts, it is important to own them and be mindful of how they progress into more extreme thoughts. An example could be when someone or multiple people cut in line at chow, the thought can start with "Who does this fool think he is?" and "Who does this guy think I am?". These thoughts can quickly progress into "I should check this fool". These unhealthy thoughts can quickly lead to confrontation and that can lead to someone getting hurt, receiving new charges, a Board denial, and many other negative consequences. It is important to catch this early so that these thoughts don't escalate and so that we can change this line of thinking, which allows us to maintain our emotions and we can disrupt these habits and develop new healthier habits. This is a really important step towards change and growth. This can have a positive impact on our quality of life as well.

CHAPTER THIRTEEN: NEW THINKING EQUALS NEW BEHAVIOR

When we change the way we think, one of the side effects, or consequences is that our behavior also changes. For many of us, this is a good thing and a needed change.

A new way of thinking has to be developed. Our thought patterns are habits just the same as our behavior. When we develop unhealthy thinking habits, but fail to admit or even realize we are doing it it just seems normal and we believe the rest of the world thinks the same way.

So, in order to change these old thinking habits we have to challenge them. What if we just ask the questions: "What if my way of thinking is wrong?" and "What if there is a healthier way?". Is it possible that you've been wrong for years, if not your entire life? Is there a chance you could have a better life if you found new ways to think about life?

What if you could wake up tomorrow to the perfect life? What would it look like? Who would be part of it? Would it look different than your life now? If that life looks different than the one you've been living, then you must change the way you have been thinking and develop new thoughts and patterns.

Some of the negative thinking habits we develop as criminals are: extreme thinking, labeling others, generalizing responses, minimizing our actions, being a martyr in our own eyes, playing the role of a victim, and putting thoughts and intentions into the minds of others that do not really exist.

CHAPTER FOURTEEN: YOU ARE WHAT YOU THINK

You are what you think. This means that however you think is how you will live. Your thinking will determine and define your goals.

If you are thinking about drugs and alcohol, you are most likely going to use drugs and alcohol. If you think about talking crazy to people and having conflict, that is what you are going to do. If you think about controlling people, or pushing them away, what do you think is going to happen?

If we live with self-doubt, and set limits for ourselves by saying we can't change we can't grow into the person we want to be, then we are usually right. This is something we must change! We must stop all the negative thinking and stop setting limits for ourselves, and transform our thinking into positive, goal-driven planning. We have to build and maintain confidence in ourselves.

Many people who have been in our situations have changed. The most important part of change is to change the way we think. This is where it starts. Our thinking sets the tone for how we feel about what we experience. It is where we start the process of how we perceive what we experience, which is how we decide to experience it and how we respond to life. An example is: If I see a couple of guys picking on someone, my thinking is going to decide how I feel about it and how I am going to respond. Do I think it is funny and cool, or that the victim just needs to stand up for himself? Do I think what jerks the two guys are, that they are just bullies? Do I think the whole scene is not my problem, that it's not me or someone

I care about getting picked on? Do I get angry and confront the bullies? Do I feel compassion for the victim? Do I feel compassion for the bullies because I understand that they are damaged on the inside and don't know any better? A combination of these thoughts, or something else? There are so many options, yet what we choose as our response is one of the ways we define ourselves and our values. This is what our thinking does for us, it leads to how we act, to our decision making.

In the past, we have spent so much time thinking about negative, unproductive things, that that is who and what we became. We became angry, hateful people who did not have any quality relationships in our life. We had no direction, no goals, and no idea who we were or who we wanted to be. We were impulsive people who made a lot of really bad decisions that have had disastrous consequences. This was all due to our wrong thought process.

We conceived of things only in a criminal and addictive way. We would think in extremes, and our responses were extreme. The slightest perception on our part of someone trying to be aggressive or disrespectful to us would result in our going over the top in response. We believed this to be normal behavior! It obviously isn't, and caused us not to trust others. How could we when we just knew they could not trust us? This led to us isolating ourselves, and also led us to begin writing scripts and contracts for ourselves.

We would script situations out in our minds and that always led to conflict and violence. In our mind, it was the only option, it was the only way things could play out. He would say this, I would say that; he does this and I do that. This thinking almost always had us escalating the situation and being the aggressor. This script thinking led us to making a contract with ourselves. "I'm not going to let this dude get away with…" or "If this dude gets crazy or loud with me I'm going to…." These contracts always led to aggression and/or violence, and they left us with no other option because we never spent any time thinking about any other options. So, we left ourselves with a limited response option, and no other skills when it came to dealing with conflict or uncomfortable situations.

The time you spend thinking a certain way is valuable, it determines how you will respond, who you are, and what your values are. We have to be mindful of how we think. We can't just let our thinking go unchecked, it needs to be something we spend a lot of time focusing on when we are changing our lives. Sitting and ruminating on something – thinking about it over and over – is an unhealthy thinking pattern where we often escalate bad experiences. This is a habit that needs to be broken. When this starts, it is important to recognize it and to focus on something else. Focus on something positive, or funny, or fun. Thinking of family and erstwhile goals are good distractions. Once some time has passed, and we have calmed down, it is okay to revisit the problem with the goal of finding a healthy solution. Don't get worked up again, but rather find an acceptable solution.

The way we think is the hardest part of change. This is where the real and true challenges lay. When we are trying to effect change it is our thinking that can trigger our guilt, self-doubt, desires, obstacles, or if we choose to think positively, this can lead the way to good opportunities.

We can choose to see these challenges as an opportunity to grow and become a better version of ourselves. A chance to reach our highest possible self. Even when we get frustrated, we don't allow those feeling to escalate. We look to practice being the person we say we are, that we want to be, to grow and make these challenges easier the next time we have to deal with them. These are our opportunities in life to fulfill our purpose.

The mindset is important. How do you choose to see things? How do you choose to experience things? How do you choose to react or respond to things? This is important because, after enough time, effort and experience, this will become your new normal … it will become who you are.

These decisions are where our values are determined. Is it okay to steal? Is it okay to hit someone? Is the use of drugs okay? Is it okay to lie? Is it okay to be lazy? These are all values we need to make decisions on. What are your values… right now? What do you want them to be? How important are healthy, pro-social values to you? Do you want to spend the time that is needed, the effort necessary, to develop healthy pro-social values? The process is hard at times, but it is incredibly rewarding too. Plus, it leads to a much better life, now, and in the future.

For many of us our identity for many years has been that of a criminal, gangster, drug abuser, alcoholic, dead beat or any other number of negative identifiers. After enough time has passed with this as our identity, we embraced it, and maybe even decided to live up to it with all that we could. Now is the time to develop a new identity and to embrace it with the same energy and commitment we have with the old identity.

This is where it is important to admit to yourself who you really want to be. You need to let go of your role as Joe Convict and begin to feed and develop your authentic, true self. We can become and be who we truly want to be.

This decision and change is not easy, but it can lead to happiness, joy, healthy relationships that are rewarding and satisfying. If we can change how we think about ourselves, we will change how we feel about ourselves. This will change how we act, treat others, treat ourselves, our values, principles and the overall quality of our lives.

CHAPTER FIFTEEN: PERSONAL PURPOSE

Live on purpose, with purpose. Stop and think about that for a minute. What does that mean to you? Not on a surface level, but on a deeper, more meaningful level.

How can you live on purpose with purpose? What values, morals and behaviors would living with purpose include? What would living like this look like? How would you like it to look? How would you like people to see this in your life?

Most people would not recognize this way of living, yet they would know that something was different. This way of living requires you to have direction and meaning in your life. This requires more than just surviving life or living day by day. To just do what is expected is not good enough if you are living on purpose with purpose. This way of living means you are concerned about more than just yourself.

We can determine what our own personal purpose is. This requires a lot of self-reflection and the examination of who and what we want to be. How many people want to be drug abusers, criminals, absent as parents, sons, spouses, uncles, etc.?

How many want to be sober, good parents that are present, have a good job, have a home and not a cell, helping rather than hurting people, or to be free from addiction and prison?

Finding our personal purpose can help us to achieve these goals.

Who would like to be a good influence on others? Their kids, friends, neighbors, co-workers, siblings? Who wants to be a good example for these same people?

Do you doubt that you can be this person? Will you let defects or insecurities get in the way of finding and living your purpose? Finding our purpose can lead to liking ourselves and developing our self-confidence, self-worth, self-esteem and it can improve our quality of life and lead to true happiness.

When we find our purpose and pursue it, it can lead to making amends, which has great value. Making amends is a very rewarding and gratifying act and can accelerate growth.

When we change from an anti-social to a pro-social lifestyle, we have a debt to repay to society that requires us to have meaning and purpose in our lives. It can start with small things, such as, no longer being a lazy liar who avoids responsibility, to big things, like, preventing the victimization of others, or being an agent of social change. It can also mean finding what really makes you happy. True joy in what you are doing in your life from choices you make are unmatched, even by drugs and alcohol. This true joy helps to reaffirm your self-worth, it signals that you are going in the right direction in your life. It's part of your moral compass.

I have determined that my purpose is to help prevent the victimization of others. My purpose is to help change people's lives so that they no longer make choices that lead to the violation of another person. By educating others, and sharing the things that I have learned, by trying to be a positive example in the way that I live my life and in the way that I treat others, by working at being a positive influence through encouragement and support of the changes that others make, and, finally, by the positive, healthy choices I make in my own life, I am living out my purpose.

It was not easy to find my purpose in life, and to learn how to live it. There was a lot of doubt. I doubted that I was capable of living such a life. How could I go from an angry, hateful, insecure, uneducated, immature, lazy, lying victimizer, to a person of integrity, compassion, empathy, patience, kindness and helpfulness? It amazes me still.

Yet, I have done it. I continue to do it, to strive and work at it each day to live with purpose in some way. Just changing and not victimizing others was not enough for me. I want to be an agent of social change, impacting society in a positive and healthy way. These are lofty goals I have set for myself, yet I owe it to anyone and everyone I have ever victimized in my life. This is how I try to balance out all the harm I have caused. There is never going to be true balance and it may be something that I may never be able to achieve. However, I will continue to try, to continue chasing that balance. This life purpose and its important meaning is an avenue of Amends for me.

Through the making of amends, and living with purpose, greater self-worth and self-confidence is gained. These gains are not to be taken lightly. This new-found view of ourselves allows us to set loftier goals, and choose bigger dreams. It allows us to treat ourselves better, which means we will treat others better. Purpose and meaning give us the ability to live a better and more fulfilling life. It allows us to live out in the open, in the light of day instead of hiding our actions in the dark, living with shame.

Living with purpose is fulfilling, empowering, and liberating. How would this impact your life? How would it impact your families? How would it impact your community? Imagine that you CAN impact people's lives in a healthy way, bring them joy instead of dread or fear.

How would that make you feel about yourself? How would you feel about the way that others now viewed you as that sort of capable person?

We don't have to think that we must be perfect. We've just got to make a true, heartfelt effort.

CHAPTER SIXTEEN: AUTHENTIC SELF

Your authentic-self ties in with your purpose. Your authentic self is who you really and truly are. Not the person you present yourself to be when you want people to like you or respect you; not the mask you present yourself as, but the real person behind the mask.

It is easy to present ourselves in different situations or different environments as a different person. At home with our family we are one way, with our friends another, at work with strangers, we are yet another way. Over time we develop these character traits that are maladaptive and unhealthy, that is not who we truly are inside. This becomes habit. Pretty soon we are no longer living our lives as our authentic self.

We present ourselves as angry or crazy or indifferent to others, and soon we are exactly that. This way of thinking and lifestyle leads us to being okay with creating victims, breaking our commitments, doing drugs, committing crimes and putting our lives and the lives of others at risk with unhealthy and flawed behavior. This too, is not our authentic self.

Your true authentic-self is the person you most desire to be, but somewhere along the way, we did not act to set goals to become that person. To become this true self, you need to be aware of the 'who' and 'what' you want to be. Do you wish to be kind? Compassionate? Caring? Spend some time thinking about this. None of us want to be drug addicts, failures in life or victimizers. Not really. We have developed unhealthy habits that have led us to these sorts of lifestyles by our not setting proper goals and finding our true purpose.

So, figure out what those habits are that you previously developed in your life that have led you to these lifestyles. Ask yourself: When did you begin to develop this way of thinking, this habit? Are you lazy? Are you a manipulator? Are you a purposeful liar? How do these and/or other bad habits keep you from being your authentic self?

What goals can you set to break away from these habits and move towards your authentic self? There are two types of goals: Short-term goals and long-term goals. Both will help you.

The short-term goals are those that can be completed now in the immediate present. These goals can answer a small, pressing need in the extant moment. Short term goals can be set so they can help prevent you from making impulsive, irrational decisions that will lead to negative consequences. These goals can also help you be aware of how you are feeling, how you are coping, in the present moment. Thus, you should be able, because of this self-awareness, to make deliberate choices to move in a positive and healthy direction.

An example of this would be: If someone tells an off-color joke about race or sexuality that offends you; instead of becoming angry and acting out or saying something wrong yourself, you have the opportunity to make a solid decision in a positive way to act in a responsible and mature way. Being aware of how this joke makes you feel ... hurt, angry, offended, embarrassed, is being in tune with your authentic self. Knowing this helps you respond in a healthy way, instead of acting impulsively, or going against who you want to be. The impulsive action could lead to regret, remorse, shame, guilt, or other negative consequences. Such as time in prison.

A long-term goal is set with short term goals to help achieve it. A long-term goal could be something like graduating college, getting out of prison, or having a family. Short term goals are needed in order to accomplish these goals.

A short-term goal can be to figure out who and what we want to be, to find our personal purpose, or to identify our authentic self. A long-term goal could be a path to becoming this person, with short term goals set up to help measure the progress being made.

Our authentic self is part of our identity that we live with when we give up the mask of who we wanted people to think we were or see us as. No longer do we let other people's opinions direct or dictate our beliefs or behaviors, but we rest on our opinions of ourselves. Your opinion of yourself should carry more weight and value than other's opinion of you.

"My opinion of me is more important than your opinion of me"

If we are living with the need of approval of other criminals, then we are not being our authentic self. We should live for ourselves and for those we love and value, who also love and value us. Learn to do things that help you develop a higher opinion of yourself. Learn to do things that cultivate your self-worth, self-respect, self-esteem, and your belief that you can achieve more than you gave yourself credit for in the past.

CHAPTER SEVENTEEN: EMOTIONAL MATURITY

What is emotional maturity? It is the ability to deal with your emotions in a mature way. Emotional maturity is the ability to deal with both positive and negative emotions in a healthy, appropriate, and productive manner.

As criminals and drug addicts, we have developed inappropriate habits that result in unacceptable behavior. One example of this is our response to anger when it surfaces. When we get angry, we over-react. We get loud and aggressive, and become abusive. Even if this abusive behavior is just words, neglect, or the threat of violence, it is still abuse.

Emotional maturity is being able to get angry, yet not act out, not act in an aggressive manner. This means we can get angry, but still make sane, rational decisions. We can work through our anger and process it so that we do not react in an impulsive manner. Emotional maturity is the ability to deal with uncomfortable emotions and confrontational situations or words in a non-confrontational way ourselves.

Anger has been corrupted by most of us through addictive thinking habits. It has become a cure-all for many of us, acting as our default emotional switch. This means when we feel embarrassed or ashamed, or feeling as if we don't belong, we will oft-times allow ourselves to feel anger instead. We do this because we don't really understand many of the other emotions that have come over us. We can't put labels on them, let alone define or describe them, so we go to our default emotion, anger, which falsely enables us to not feel weak, vulnerable, embarrassed or any other uncomfortable emotion.

By developing emotional maturity, we can begin to understand how we are really feeling and are able to act on those feelings in an appropriate and mature manner. One important aspect of emotional maturity is developing the ability to recognize how we are feeling in any given situation. How do you feel when people are laughing at you? It's not anger. That is a secondary response emotion. Are you embarrassed? Why are you feeling that way? What thoughts trigger this response? Emotional maturity gives us the ability to process how we are truly feeling and work through these times of discomfort. These experiences are momentary and will pass. There is no need to compound the problem by acting out in an inappropriate way and causing ourselves more distress.

Anger appears to be a safe place for many of us, providing escape from being vulnerable and being overwhelmed by the emotions we have mostly been able to ignore for the majority of our lives. Anger allows us to cover these other emotions, and once we get angry, the feeling only escalates, never diminishes. Then we get angrier because we feel we have let others and ourselves down. So, we become defensive, finger-point and cast blame, and direct our attention to something or someone else so that we don't have to own or explain how we are really feeling. Now we are backed into a safe, dark, corner of anger, and we defend our anger with more anger; which only gives us the illusion of being safe or in control.

In all reality, anger, for the most part, is a destructive emotion, especially for relationships, and our own well-being. It is a form of emotional blackmail in relationships with friends and family. We keep such rigid lines drawn in our lives, so uncompromising, that no one can cross them without experiencing our anger and denunciation. So much so that people we care about cannot be themselves, and this is what is damaging to the relationship. That is true blackmail … 'don't cross the line or else!'

Emotional maturity allows us to develop the skillset to deal with the challenges of life. Where we would previously go into a rant, cussing, screaming, or being emotionally immature and over-reacting to something, we can now maintain our self-control and not respond by acting out, which only serves to escalate the situation. Emotional maturity is the ability to just sit in the moment, be uncomfortable if necessary, for a few minutes, breathe and let the problem dissolve away. A couple of deep breaths later, we can respond like a mature adult. We are not children with wet diapers who need to cry and yell to get a change.

This type of change does not take place overnight. It is a process that requires us to continually practice being mindful of how we are feeling, and how we are expressing those feelings. When we are caught up in an uncomfortable situation that triggers uncomfortable emotions, pay attention to how you are feeling. Not the anger, but the emotion that is under or behind the anger. Learn about what emotions make you most uncomfortable, and develop the skills to counter these feelings in a healthy and mature way.

One way to accomplish this is acceptance of the way you are feeling. Tell yourself that it's okay to be embarrassed. Everyone feels it, so what is the big deal? Just ride it out for a few minutes, and soon it's gone. If we make a big scene and get angry, it compounds the problem by inserting all new issues that we will have to deal with later. Issues such as: Apologies and explanations, lost relationships, or being held accountable by the legal system – consequences we don't like and can live without.

Emotional maturity will also allow us to deal with the ups and downs of life instead of running to drugs or alcohol to mask the problem, which only further deteriorates our emotional maturity and stability, leading to more unhealthy emotional habits. Emotional maturity gives us the ability to deal with life in a safe, productive, healthy way, one that adds to our quality of life and gives richness to our relationships.

If we are living in a healthy, mature way, we won't have to spend time repairing our relationships, and can instead, nurture them and grow them in a healthy and fulfilling way. We can have peace instead of worrying about how to "fix" the wrongs we have done, and this will have a ripple effect on our loved ones. They too, then, can have a happier and healthier life. This alone should be motivation enough for us.

Begin by monitoring how you act when you are angry, or not getting your way. Are you acting out by getting loud, breaking things, or something else along those lines? If you are, come up with some healthy ways to respond instead. We have to admit to ourselves that this type of behavior is a problem in our lives and it is unacceptable.

A big step for many of us is to give up "Right Fighting". This is not a mature habit! It is counter-productive and damages our relationships. Arguing to be right is just an attempt to control, save face, or some other immature need to feed one's ego and be right. Two people can disagree on something without one person proving to the other that they are wrong, or forcing them to agree or to see things your way. It's okay to disagree; it does not mean someone is dumb or a lesser person, it's just a disagreement. Don't make it more than that with an argument. Be the mature one and let it go.

People who are consistent with their personality and don't have a lot of ups and downs, are considered emotionally mature. They don't have to express how they are feeling with extreme behavior. These people usually have good, high quality relationships that are rewarding. To be consistent is a great goal. A consistent person attracts others to them who are also consistent, and that creates a calmer lifestyle, which is easier to maintain than a chaotic one that is immature in its ups and down. One of the rewards of a life of emotional maturity is consistency in relationships.

In the process of learning all these new skills we develop a certain sense of accomplishment, one that will uplift and encourage us. We unlearn our past bad habits. There is no emergency that we must respond to right now. Strive to not behave in an unhealthy way, but rather look for new ways to express yourself assertively while still being respectful of another's viewpoint. Show respect and appreciate the respect reflected back to you. Stand still in the moment, own your feelings, label them, and use them to progress in your understanding of yourself. Learn to decrease the negative and increase the positive. Have the thought that your emotions are yours to control, not the other way around. Realize that you do not always need to defend your position in life as if that is the most important thing. Being at peace with yourself and others, especially those you love and care about, far supersedes the need to be right. Living your life, always being on the defensive is very tiring emotionally, taxing you and wearing you down. Embrace difference. Embrace emotional maturity as a life-saving measure, as it surely can be. Grow then into your highest possible self.

CHAPTER EIGHTEEN: VICTIMIZATION

When we begin to admit to what we have done when it comes to creating victims, it will, without a doubt, be very uncomfortable. Admitting how we have negatively impacted people's lives by our selfish decisions and actions is a very hard thing to do. It is difficult to admit to being wrong and to be honest in our self-appraisal. These are not good things that we are recognizing about ourselves, so the honesty will be brutal to absorb. Our past misdeeds are not something that we are proud of. Many of us have spent a large part of our lives glorifying our crimes, bragging and showing off about the hurtful things done to others. Many of us did this because we felt that it earned us, or gained us, some greater measure of respect from our peers.

These behaviors became habit, and then became normal, after having done them enough. When we start to admit and realize that these behaviors are not at all normal, it will be embarrassing and shamefully uncomfortable for some of us. These are hard things to deal with, but it is possible to go through the moment and end up feeling good about the direction our lives have taken. Again, change is not easy, but the results are worth the effort. The rewards are numerous.

The more we learn about how our actions impact others, the real and long-lasting implications, the more we should want to change. The more we should accept those feelings will be a challenge because of the very fact that they are so uncomfortable to recall and admit. We have spent considerable time and effort pushing such feelings away, stuffing them, denying and ignoring them. These challenges can make our going back to our old ways seem inviting because they are easy and comfortable. We must challenge this. We must stay the course.

The long-lasting effects we have on people's lives can be widespread. There are many different areas of people's lives that are affected by being the victim of a crime.

A person is affected by crime physically, emotionally, financially, and spiritually. Take some time to make a list of some ways that a person may show an effect of being victimized by crime. Think about how different crimes effect people. Think about how your crime(s) affected others. What are the results? How has your victim, or victims, been impacted? This is intended as a hard exercise, but it is one that is needed so that we as victimizers can better understand our impact on people's lives. There are NO victimless crimes. Everyone involved suffers. Think about who could be listed as victims of your crimes.

In thinking about the impact of crime on victims, consider this: How are holidays effected? Birthdays, weddings, anniversaries? Births or graduation? Promotions in a job? How are our crimes affecting people and their lives years later? Some victims never completely heal. They suffer the effects of crime for the rest of their lives. Each crime has its own unique impact on a person's life. Think about the victims of your crime(s), and how their lives are doing. How do you think they felt at the moment of the crime? How about your arrest? Your trial and sentencing? How did they feel going through those events? How were their families impacted? Use words to describe what they possibly went through, what they experienced. Find and use words other than 'hurt or scared'. What else did they feel? How does it make them feel to recall the event, or, think about you getting out of prison?

This is a serious issue. Many people, in fact most, that are in prison are going to be released. How does this impact our victims and their families? Many of them might succumb to the fear at the thought of your release, even if the crime occurred ten or twenty or even thirty years ago. The crime and the resultant fear and/or pain becomes real again. They are scared. In their mind, we are still the same person that hurt them or their family. Think about it. They, more than anyone else, should have nothing to fear from us. Can we understand this? It is within our grasp to do so by the use of a vital and important feeling, empathy. We need to learn it, develop it, and understand how it can effect change in our lives. Learn it so that we can at last understand our victims, and use this knowledge to change our own behavior.

CHAPTER NINETEEN: FOCUSING OUR ENERGY

Where are your energies focused? Are they only focused on making problems worse, or are they concentrated of fixing problems? Do you spend more of your time and energy on feeding irrational, hostile, angry, aggressive or violent thoughts? Do you ruminate on perceived wrongs? Do you look for a reasonable explanation why someone did or said something "out of pocket"? Where are your energies focused?

Many of us are conflict-driven, often on the lookout for some area of conflict we might get ourselves involved in. We play at assuming that this or that person said or did something as a way to insult, disrespect, or embarrass us. We automatically become confrontational, and prepare ourselves for conversations, but with negative thoughts prompting us. There are many easy and healthy ways to resolve conflict before it begins. We just need to discover what they are and develop the skills necessary to practice them in our lives. Finding and developing these skills helps us learn to focus our energies in a healthy way.

What are some of these skills, and how can we use them, especially to resolve conflict? If you cannot answer this question right at this moment, that's okay. The truth is, you already have some of the answers, you are just not realizing it … yet. If you feel as if you don't have any answers at all, find someone whom you believe may have some good ideas about where to look. Ask them. Don't worry, they'll understand. It is okay to seek help and advice. This is not weakness, but rather smart thinking.

Some of us seem to need conflict. We receive a feeling of self-worth, however fleeting and short-lived it is, from conflict. When we jump into a conflict situation it is important for us to "win", which then reinforces the feeling of self-worth. This self-worth is valueless and will disappear eventually, to be replaced by our insecurities.

Occasionally we win a few of these conflicts, therefore we feel good about ourselves, and we brag or show-off. We tell ourselves, "Yeah, I did that!" This does not last however, as it is not real, not a true essence of self-worth, self-esteem or self-confidence. Conflict, win lose or draw, is ultimately a negative thing.

When we learn to deal with hard situations in a mature and appropriate way is when we begin to get a true sense of self-worth. To resolve a problem ensuring both sides are happy, feel that their needs have been met, and not feel that they have been bullied into a conclusion they are not sure of, is an ideal outcome. This is possible. We can learn how to do this. Also, just because the other person wants to have conflict or confrontation does not mean we have to give in, match their anger with our own, or fall into their behavioral mode. We can choose to respond in a healthy and mature way. This is the when and how we employ our learned coping skills.

Active listening skills are an effective way to deal with and avoid conflict. What are active listening skills? They are the application of the "two and one concept". We have one mouth which to speak, but two ears to really listen. If we listen attentively, showing respect as we do, this allows the speaker to feel valued as they are heard. They feel relief at being listened to. Don't we all want that? To have someone really listen? These skills can involve directly facing the other person, making appropriate eye contact, verbal affirmations, and restating what the other person has said. This confirms to them that you were paying attention. These skills apply in all areas of life, and in all relationships.

One issue that may arise when we find ourselves in these situations is that we have a tendency to be busy trying to formulate our response – what we want to say – instead of actively listening to the person. We also need to avoid talking 'over' the other individual. This is not only frustrating, it can lead to anger and conflict, which is what we are trying to avoid. Arguments begin and the situation becomes negative and unfavorable.

Important also is awareness of your body language. Are you appearing agitated or angry? Do you show yourself as frustrated or in a hurry? Be aware of this. Try very hard to remain calm and relaxed, giving the other person your full attention. Stand relaxed, with your arms uncrossed, your hands casual and loose. Make eye contact, smile and nod in agreement. All important.

This is about relationships. What value do you place on your own relationships? How do you want your relationships to be defined? These are important questions to consider. When we find ourselves having a lot of conflict and confrontation in our lives, we should acknowledge that we ourselves are the common denominators. We are the one person that is constant and involved in each of these situations. It is our responsibility to change in order to avoid conflict. It is our choice. How do you want to be viewed, thought of and talked about? Do you want people to like and admire you for your calmness and restraint? Do people want to be around you, or do they avoid you? Do you want to have healthy, rewarding relationships that are strong and enduring or do you desire to continue having conflict in your life?

These skills are not always easy to obtain or to practice right off the bat, but by sticking to it, the endeavors become less troublesome and more pleasurable. They become easier with time, our lives become better, more rewarding and healthier, both physically and emotionally. The time and effort required to develop these skills are worth it, and your overall quality of life will improve.

CHAPTER TWENTY: RELAPSE PREVENTION PLANNING

To be efficiently prepared to re-enter society, we need to have an effective Relapse Prevention Plan. Such a plan requires brutal self-honesty.

A truly good Relapse Prevention Plan is found through deep self-reflection that is fearless and honest. This self-reflection will allow us to admit our weaknesses as well as find our strengths, and knowing both is the basis for a good Relapse Prevention Plan.

Knowing our weaknesses allows us to recognize the dangers of relapse, and from where they may spring up for us. We all have many similar trigger areas but we also have many things that are solely ours and unique to us. So, copying someone else's plan may work on the surface, but it will not hold up under scrutiny. This is why it is important that YOU do the work.

Finding our triggers is a starting point. What could cause you to relapse into old behaviors? These behaviors may range from drug or alcohol use, to anger and violence, they can also include gambling, sex, desire for fast money or any other behavior that is problematic or maladaptive (bad). Knowing what triggers any or all of these things is important because knowledge can help us to avoid or cope with these triggers.

Let's start with substance use. What triggers your desire to use? This desire is dangerous because it can easily become a craving and cravings turn into a lapse and a lapse may turn into a relapse. So, what types of events can cause you to want to use? There are an endless number of triggers, both internal (our thinking and emotions) and external (people, places and things).

The internal can start with a thought, one example could be, "I can never stop using". This one, single thought can lead to other thoughts that create desire and eventually a craving that is difficult to manage. These types of thoughts are precursors which are ways to start down the path to giving ourselves permission to use. This is why a Relapse Prevention Plan is so important, it shows that we are aware of the danger areas, and we recognize how small things can become big things.

These thoughts can also trigger emotions we have a difficult time managing. The thought, "I can never stop using", can trigger a laundry list of emotions such as feeling like a failure or fraud, insecurity, anger, resentment or a number of other negative emotions. The awareness of how these thoughts impact us and how we respond to them is how we learn to manage what we are going through. We can go through many things in life that could trigger a possible relapse, however, if we are prepared to understand what we are experiencing and how to best navigate these rough waters, a relapse is much less likely, hence the need for a personalized Relapse Prevention Plan.

For some of us, there are many internal triggers, such as stuffing our feelings, isolating ourselves, loneliness, negative thinking, procrastination, etc. Figuring out how to manage these feelings and behaviors is what can take us from anti-social to pro-social behavior and may lead to a possible finding of suitability by the Board at future hearings.

The list and examples given here are by no means complete, so take time to find out what your personal triggers are and how they influence your thinking, your decision making, and your behavior so that you can speak about them in an open and honest way when you need to.

External triggers we have less control over. We cannot control anything outside of ourselves. However, recognizing them is just as important.

One of the main reasons people come back to prison is their inability to get a job. So not being able to get a job or losing one's job is a big trigger. This can lead to many negative thoughts and feelings, which can lead to poor choices being made. Not being able to find a job or losing a job can lead to an attitude of quitting or giving up, which can lead to the compromising of our values, morals, and beliefs by stealing or selling drugs. "All of a sudden, I don't have a job and can't pay my bills", which a "man" is supposed to be able to do, so, now it starts to become acceptable to go steal a couple of things to help pay the rent. These bad choices lead to more bad choices such as "I'll just sell a little dope". Now we are exposing ourselves to drugs in an intimate way which leads us to lying and being secretive. This can also lead us to using which comes with an entirely new set of problems and bad decisions.

So, being honest with ourselves about what our triggers are and how they can impact us is important because it allows us to build a plan to manage these triggers or stressors.

Other external triggers can be loud, aggressive people, having no place to live, bars, liquor stores, drugs, alcohol, or gang members. This is not a complete list, but it is a starting point to find out what some of your triggers and stressors are.

Now that we have an idea of what our triggers are and how they can impact us, we need to figure out how to cope with these triggers or how we can best manage them. There are as many ways to cope with life's triggers as there are triggers. Not all coping strategies will work for everyone. There are a lot of common coping skills that people like to use, such as, talking to someone, journaling, listening to music, prayer, attending meetings, working on a hobby, or practicing meditation. These are all good and they can all be helpful. The key is to find what works for you and understand why it is an important coping skill for you. What does this particular coping strategy do for you?

For me, playing with a dog always sounds like a good way to deal with stress and refocus my energies. A dog is not judgmental, it does not share its problems with me and it just wants to have fun. This is a way for me to burn energy while I process what I am feeling and thinking. This allows for some time and distance between what triggered me and when I make a decision; this way I am not making an impulsive decision. Playing with a dog can also allow me to create some positive self-talk which is important for me when I am going through hard times or dealing with stressful situations. I can decompress and refocus myself. Such steps lead to success.

A substance abuse Relapse Prevention Plan is probably one of the most common forms of self-rehab we have to use in prison. Most of us have abused drugs or alcohol or both at one point or another in our lives. When we sit and reflect on our lives in an open and honest way, we can begin to figure out why we started to use substances. We can learn what our motives were when we started and we can address these issues, and we can shape our relapse prevention plans around these things, these insecurities, these weaknesses or defects that motivated our substance use.

Our coping skills should be focused on things that help us navigate our lives in a productive and healthy way. Our substance abuse is just a coping skill that we think helps us deal with the real problems in our lives. Substance use is about avoiding pain or seeking pleasure so that we don't have to deal with the reality of our lives. Instead of dealing with the fact that we have an absent father and how that makes us feel or think about ourselves, we turn to substances to avoid those negative thoughts and feelings, or we use them to avoid dealing with how we think others view us.

Coping skills and exercises that help us build self-esteem, self-confidence or self-worth are very helpful because these are real values and they help us to endure the hardships of life instead of running from them and getting high or drunk. Good ways to build these things up in our lives is to do good things for others, such as volunteering your time at a church or shelter, or animal shelters or doing things to help the disadvantaged. These are things that make us feel better about ourselves and that makes doing the right thing more attractive to us.

Our social circle is extremely important to our sobriety and to our decision-making, so, we must be aware of who we spend our time with. When we choose to spend our time with people who are engaged in criminal behavior, we become accepting of criminal behavior, and creating victims becomes okay. This should not be who we spend time with, so, our Relapse Prevention Plans should reflect this and engage us in positive and healthy activities.

When we volunteer our time to help other people, we are most likely making their lives better, and in all likelihood, they will express gratitude. This gratitude can help us to feel better about ourselves and motivate us to do more because it feels good. It is a rewarding and a noble way to spend our time.

In 12-step programs, step 12 speaks of being of service, it says "Here we experience the kind of giving that asks no rewards". (Twelve Steps and Twelve Traditions Alcoholics Anonymous World Services, Inc.) We ask for no rewards because the reward is the act itself. The feeling of doing good and doing right is in and of itself rewarding. There is true satisfaction from doing kind things for others with nothing expected in return. These acts can add to a person's sense of self-worth and can be built upon to help motivate further growth.

These selfless acts can help to develop a sense of identity as well. Who and what we see ourselves as can greatly influence our behavior, and doing and being good helps to build a healthy self-identity. We can go from seeing ourselves as strong, independent people who think the world owes us something, to kind and compassionate, helpful people that understand that we do have something good to offer the world.

Our Relapse Prevention Plans do not just keep us from relapsing, they can also help us grow into the person we are supposed to be, they help us represent our highest possible self. This helps us grow into the version of ourselves that is less and less likely to relapse, because dealing with life's ups and downs become easier and doing the right thing becomes more and more a part of who we are. It becomes our authentic self.

CHAPTER TWENTY-ONE: RELAPSE PREVENTION PLAN-ANGER MANAGEMENT

There is a specific need for an Anger Management Relapse Prevention Plan for almost all of us who are incarcerated. Many of us have corrupted the natural emotion of anger. We have turned anger into an all-purpose emotion. Many of us have done this because we never developed the understanding of what we are actually feeling or experiencing and have automatically filed these emotions under anger. We are doing ourselves a disservice by doing this, we are cheating ourselves

TRIGGERS

While sitting in Anger Management classes, I have often times heard people say, "I don't get angry." Really? Is this a lack of honesty or a lack of self-knowledge? We all experience anger, most likely on a daily basis. Irritation, annoyance, frustration and irksomeness are all mild forms of anger. Anger is not a bad emotion to feel, it tells us something is wrong, warns us to pay attention, and lets us know that our needs are not being met. The issue is how often or intensely we get angry and what we do with that anger. This is part of the way we have corrupted anger. We use it far too often to get our way, to feel safe, to control others, to avoid responsibility, to intimidate others, and a number of other misuses. There are much more effective ways for us to communicate.

When I was younger I would experience emotions that I could not describe or understand, and that would cause me to not know what to do or why I felt the way I felt. Even as an adult in prison this continued to be true, so I would hit my default button and go to what I knew and trusted, anger.

When I would feel emotions such as guilt, embarrassment, loneliness, or shame, I would not understand them fully and that would make me more uncomfortable, so I would embrace anger as my go-to emotion. This became a habit and led to me becoming aggressive and violent. When I was embarrassed or feeling guilty and I would become angry, it was as if whatever was making me feel that way would cease for the moment. I no longer had to feel more of those feelings. I would instead become angrier and that was a much safer emotion to me. Anger became an emotion of power, other emotions made me feel weak and/or vulnerable, but not anger.

This is just one, among many, examples of how we corrupt anger. To recognize what our anger looks and feels like, where it comes from and how to manage it, it is important to explore some of this in order to learn what is essential for our personal Relapse Prevention Plans. Remember, personalize your plans and know them, be able to talk about them. Your story may not be like my story, but you have an anger story that is yours you should reflect on it and understand it so that you can better manage it. This work and understanding will make the quality of your life better.

An Anger Relapse Prevention Plan has three key areas. People, places, and things. It is important to know yourself and how you get triggered, how your warning signs express themselves, and how you can best manage or cope with your anger.

We will start with triggers. Another way to describe triggers is by calling them stressors. Either way, they are what cause us to respond with anger. Triggers have two categories, the first one being internal. These are the ones that reside inside of us, our thoughts and emotions. Since these are inside of us, we have more control over them. The second category is external triggers, other people, places and things. We cannot control these things; however, we can control our responses to them. To recognize the differences and to be able to identify exactly what is triggering us, is crucial, because we can then decide how to effectively cope with and manage our anger.

Internal triggers are often about ourselves, our circumstances, our lives or our experiences. Among other things, you must spend time thinking about your anger so that you can figure out and discover where it comes from.

Negative thinking can lead to anger. When we think in negative terms all the time or even some of the time it can lead to us becoming frustrated or resentful, and that can directly lead to anger. Think about the way you think. Is there negativity in your thoughts? Are you judgmental towards others? Do you put people down a lot, think about how they should be, or what they should do, or how they should do something? Do you expect people to be the way you believe is right and if they don't live by your standards or ways, do you criticize them in your thoughts? Do you think in extremes? Do you think "all" people are a certain way? Do you think things "always" or "never" go a certain way? Do you think that "nothing" "ever" goes your way? Do you think that "everyone" in society is against you? These are all examples of extreme thinking, which is a form of negative thinking and this creates an unhealthy way of living. This type of thinking can lead to a lot of unresolved anger.

Loneliness can lead to anger. Loneliness is a source of anger for a lot of people in prison, I believe. I have heard many people talk about this. Loneliness can lead to self-pity or depression and that is hard for a macho man to admit, so we avoid dealing with those "weak" emotions and we focus on being angry instead. We can become short-tempered and impatient with people and that has the danger of escalating quickly, so we must be aware of these feelings.

Once we are released from prison and beginning to live our new lives, the feelings of loneliness and its dangers can easily follow. We may feel insecure around "normal" people or "citizens". This can make us feel isolated or alone and that could lead to thoughts of using or resentments that carry over to the next day or the next interaction. With enough of this, we might do or say something inappropriate that causes us problems. We may lose a job or the place we are staying, because we didn't stay mindful of what we were thinking or how we were feeling, and suddenly, we are headed down a slippery and dangerous slope.

If we are not aware of our thoughts and feelings, a number of things can lead to anger. We need to know ourselves, so we can recognize when we are feeling certain ways or when we are thinking in certain patterns. The more we are conscious of ourselves the better we can manage our emotions and responses. We will never live life completely anger free because it is an emotion we are born with. We just need to learn to manage our anger in a healthy and pro-social way. The more triggers we can identify, the better we will be at managing our responses to them.

There are many internal triggers. Here are just a few: negative thinking, loneliness, procrastination, boredom, isolation, stuffing feelings, lack of communication, shame, guilt, embarrassment, insecurities, self-doubt, low self-esteem and low self-worth.

Many of these are complicated thoughts and emotions, but with time and effort, you can figure them out and identify how they work in your life. Find trusted people to help you learn about these things in your life. Seek out other people's opinions on this. Be open to new ideas and learning about yourself. The better you know yourself, the easier these things are to talk about, and all these things will be talked about at Psych Evals. and at the Board. This kind of self-knowledge is difficult to come to grips with at first, but the more you push through the hard and uncomfortable parts, the better and more rewarding your life will become. The best part may be how much your relationships will improve, an awesome reward.

Learn to not only know what you're feeling or thinking, but how to describe those feelings. Being able to describe what we are going through and why, is powerful. It is something that can be liberating. To no longer be a prisoner of our thoughts and emotions is incredibly freeing and brings new options to the table for us.

Now we have covered internal triggers, let's go over some external triggers. These are the things that are outside of us and outside of our control. Let's start with people. What types of people trigger your anger? Loud people? Aggressive people? People who are rude? Criminals? Gang members? Liars? Or, are there some other types that trigger your anger? What do they do or not do that triggers your anger? Be honest with yourself, there is no reason to deny what makes you angry, admitting it will actually help you grow and change your life. What does this person do that makes you angry? Be specific. Do they gossip? Do they put you down? Try to control you? Do they not listen to you? Now, think about how this affects you. What is it about these things that cause you to get angry?

One example could be a person who is always telling me what to do. This person could micro-manage everything I do at work, constantly telling me how to do things. After a while, I might become frustrated. This frustration could lead to resentments because I am not sure how this person would respond if I were to tell them how they are making me feel. Instead of saying to them, "When you tell me what to do and how to do it, it makes me feel like you have a low opinion of my ability to do the job, like you don't trust me and these things make me feel like you think I am incompetent." Assertive communication.

By not expressing this assertive communication I am stuffing my feelings and allowing resentments to build, which will grow over time. When we are aware of how people make us feel, it allows us to process it in a healthy way and to come up with healthy resolutions, instead of an eventual outburst. There are so many different personality types we are going to encounter, some of them will annoy or frustrate us in life. Part of being a mature, well-adjusted adult is being able to deal with people we find difficult in a healthy way and not becoming aggressive or violent.

What are some other external triggers you may run into in life? How about old friends? They can be dangerous for us because they may expect us to be who we were in the past and want us to hang out. For many of us, this may not be an option. So, what if you ran into an old friend who wanted you to hang out and you refused, but your old friend keeps insisting. How would you respond? How would their pressure make you feel? Some of us may become angry and think, 'This person is not respecting my boundaries.' What if this person becomes antagonistic or hostile towards you, how would that make you feel? Would you become defensive or angry? Would you be firm? Would you remain calm and try to get out of the situation?

These types of challenges need to be thought through so we can be aware of how we would feel about such encounters. This awareness and understanding of ourselves is how we build a solid, personal Relapse Prevention Plan. This allows us to know our own truth, to be aware of it and to be prepared for when some of the tricky situations that may pop up. This helps us to decide how to deal with these challenges in an effective way. Again, spend time learning about yourself by understanding what type of people can trigger an anger response from you and why. The better you know yourself and understand these dynamics, the less people will trigger your anger.

What types of places could trigger your anger? A place where you felt an injustice against you occurred? A place where you were previously assaulted? A place where a friend or family member was hurt? An old hang-out? How about the parole office? What if you saw an old enemy there, would that cause you to become angry? Why? One reason is the uncertainty of what he/she is going to do and that can lead to fear which can easily turn to anger as a form of protection. Are you aware of any other possible scenarios that could trigger your anger? Think about high-risk places, have a plan in place for them. Preparation is crucial.

So, now onto the 'things'. What types of things can trigger anger in you? This can be a hard one for some people. How about lines? This is a common complaint that I hear about, long lines, people cutting in line, conversations overheard in line, etc. Like the lines, the list can be long. We will have to deal with lines at stores, lines at the D.M.V., lines at the Social Security office, lines at the bank, etc. Lines everywhere!

Another thing that may be frustrating is being placed on hold when we are making phone calls, trying to get our lives together. In prison, we get 15-minute phone calls, can you imagine spending those 15 minutes on hold? Some people would get frustrated. That could be a short time to be on hold for some places. Calls being transferred from one person to the next with a new explanation provided by us, needed with each new person. All these new things that we will encounter once we are released, have the potential to build up over time if we are not mindful of what we are feeling and how we are thinking.

What about trying to get a job and getting turned down time after time because we are felons? That can be hard. The impulse to quit and give up is going to be there for some of us. The feelings of rejection can lead to anger and that can build over time. Feeling hopeless can be dangerous in these situations.

How about finding a place to live? This can be a challenge for us as well. Some places just are not going to want us living there. We are a danger or liability to them. How is this rejection going to feel?

When we are prepared for these experiences and have a plan for how we intend to navigate these challenging times, we are much more likely to make good decisions and to have a positive outcome. This is what a Relapse Prevention Plan is about - being prepared. The best way for us to be prepared is to know ourselves, know what upsets us, frustrates us, annoys us, so that we can manage it before it becomes an anger situation. Don't let things build up, process them before they are expressed in an aggressive or violent manner, these responses should no longer be acceptable to us. Think about all the harm that has been done as a result of anger not being managed in a healthy and appropriate way. This is unacceptable. Make sure you are prepared.

WARNING SIGNS

Now that we have covered our triggers, let's cover what some of the warning signs are. There are four areas of warning signs: **mental, emotional, physical and behavioral**. Each of these tell us that something is wrong; if only we are paying attention. It is like the Emergency Alert System that come on the T.V. during bad weather. These are your signals to take precautions.

Mental warning signs are the ways we think. By monitoring what our thoughts are, they can tell us if we are building towards anger or an anger explosion. They also tell us if we are building resentment. Our thinking can tell us a lot about what is going on internally and give us the opportunity to address the issues before we act out. Our thinking influences everything – our emotions, physical responses, and behavioral responses. Just as we can think ourselves into bad situations, we can think ourselves out of them as well. Some of the warning signs that signal we may be having a problem can be things such as irrational thinking, compulsive thinking, ruminations, blaming others, negative self-talk, black and white thinking, rationalizing, all-or-nothing thinking, fortune telling, or mind reading. These are all signs that something needs to be addressed. There are other signs that you have most likely learned in an anger management or criminal addictive thinking class that you can include in your Relapse Prevention Plan, if they apply to you. Shape your plan and tailor it to your specific needs.

If we catch ourselves thinking in a maladaptive manner and we recognize this, we can change it. Our thinking in stressful or challenging ways is a habit. It is something we have developed and honed over time. It is how we get ourselves into bad situations and it is the way we give ourselves permission to act aggressively or violently. Our thinking primes us for these situations and can be our own worst enemy. However, our thinking can also save us or get us out of challenging situations. If we focus on changing how we think, we will act differently as well. Our options for how to deal with triggers will change. This is an important part of an anger management plan or a Relapse Prevention Plan. Be aware of it and address it.

The next area to be conscious of when it comes to warning signs is **emotional warning signs**. This is what we are feeling and how it is impacting our current situation. Sometimes our emotions are really strong and intense. For some of us, this is difficult to manage and makes us feel as if we need to do something to release the emotions. That can be dangerous. These intense emotions will pass if we can learn to relax and practice our coping skills. The intensity will diminish once we start to manage our emotions. If we deal with them properly, there is no need to act out. There are many emotional warning signs that we need to be aware of. For instance: shame, guilt, frustration, worthlessness, embarrassment, rejection, humiliation, self-consciousness, or feelings of inadequacy. These are all difficult emotions to deal with at times and can cause us to act out, if we experience them too intensely. We can learn to deal with them in a healthy way and can develop good coping skills that help us move beyond the intense feelings of those emotions.

Almost all of us have something we are ashamed of. This is a really intense emotion. When we feel shame about something, it means we also feel like there is something wrong with us. This is hard to understand and manage at times. There are many examples of this, such as: a crime committed, being the victim of rape or molestation, where we come from, being called a punk or a bitch in front of a group of peers, or being challenged to fight and doing the right thing, yet still being called names for not fighting. These things can all trigger shame.

All of these types of emotions are difficult to deal with at times, but it helps to understand what we are feeling and to have a plan on how to manage these emotions. Our emotions have made many of us act out in the past, so we need to be aware of the challenges and be prepared to handle them in a mature, healthy way. Spend some time thinking about how situations you have encountered in the past have caused you to act out and how they truly made you feel. Be honest with yourself and ask yourself questions about why you felt the way you felt and how you can do better in a similar situation. Use what you learn to help you develop a good Relapse Prevention Plan.

Physical warning signs are next. This is our body telling us there is something wrong. Listen to it, pay attention and deploy your coping skills. Our bodies are wise, they respond this way from experience. Again, there are a lot of warning signs of anger that manifest themselves in our body. Our bodies have a variety of ways to let us know there is a problem. Pay attention to what is going on with yourself physically when your anger is triggered. Does your breathing change? Some people start taking shorter, more shallow breaths. Does your heartrate increase? Do you start sweating? Do you get that feeling in your stomach, the butterflies? There are other signs that something is wrong. Pay attention to your body. Not everything can be listed, some things you need to do the work to discover, you need to find what is yours and include it in your Relapse Prevention Plan. You need to be able to talk about and describe your plans, so it is important to pay attention to all four areas of the warning signs.

Do these feelings motivate you to act out even more? These can be uncomfortable to feel, so we have taught ourselves that feeling these different warning signs means that we have to do something about it. Yes, we do have to do something about it. We must make good decisions and deal with challenges in a healthy, pro-social way. Remember, these things are signs that something is wrong, so be prepared to manage them in a mature and appropriate way. There is no need for impulsive or immature responses to stressful or challenging events in our lives, we can make good decisions. Pay attention to what your body is telling you and use the coping skills that you have in your tool belt.

Behavioral warning signs are the fourth area of our warning signs. These are the ways that we have learned to struggle with our anger. This is an outward expression of our anger. I call this the way we struggle with our anger because for many of us, we use it to intimidate or warn others that we are angry. It's a "leave me alone behavior".

Think about the signs and ask yourself why you do it, if not to warn others and intimidate them. It's not to be inviting and friendly. Some behavioral warning signs include: clenched fists, clenched jaw, staring, scrunched forehead, puffed chest, tight lips, or impulsiveness. These things scream "back up, leave me alone." This is not always the response we get, but it's usually what we want. We could act this way because we are afraid, however, we are turning that fear into anger and we need to manage that anger.

If you are being honest with yourself about these behavioral expressions, what else are you trying to do, if not warn or intimidate? You're not trying to get a date. So, think about how you behave when you get angry, what are you doing? Why are you doing these things? Do you want to change them? This is an important aspect of your Relapse Prevention Plan because it shows that you are aware of how you are acting when you get angry, and we can change our behaviors, especially if we can recognize and identify them.

We don't have to act this way. These are important warning signs because when our anger is triggered, it is usually the 'behavioral' that first alerts us since it happens so quickly. The stare or breathing happen quickly, often times, before we even realize it.

The 'behavioral', for me, was like a wake-up call when I was first learning to manage my anger. When it happened, I would realize that I needed to pay attention to what was happening. I was building myself up for a conflict, a confrontation, some aggression, or violence. Realizing this allowed me to catch my anger much quicker, before I acted impulsively, or did something I would later regret. Once I was able to catch these behaviors, I was able to learn to catch my anger by paying attention to my thinking and emotions. This meant that I could catch my anger as soon as possible, so that it did not escalate quickly. This change has allowed me to manage my life in a much healthier way. This has been extremely rewarding for me. I used to live a life filled with conflict, I used to get into a lot of physical altercations because I did not know about all of these warning signs, but now I live my life without violence or aggression and my life is much better because of it.

With time and effort, anything is possible. So, take the time, put in the effort and improve your life and your relationships.

Now that we know what triggers our anger and what the warning signs are, we need to develop coping skills for our Relapse Prevention Plan.

COPING SKILLS

Again, there are many, many different coping skills. You have to invest the time and find out which ones work best for you. You don't need a super long list of 20 different coping skills. What you need is an effective list that you can explain and personalize. How and why do they work for you? You will find that some coping skills work more effectively for you than others do.

Coping skills are what we use to deal with and manage difficult situations. Some situations are more difficult and intense than others so more skills or more advanced skills are needed. Some skills used are: deep breathing, taking a time out, walking away, actively listening to the other person, putting things into perspective, compromising, negotiating, thinking of consequences, counting to ten, challenging our thoughts, thought stopping, mindfulness, meditation, knowing I only control myself or just being kind. This is just a short list, however, it is a very effective one.

Let's start with thought challenging. When we are in a situation that is triggering our anger, we may have some pretty irrational thoughts, such as fortune telling. Thought challenging allows us to challenge these thoughts in a way that lets us realize or admit we are being irrational or unfair. If we are thinking, "This guy is never going to hire me, I'm never going to get a job anywhere, I'm not going to be able to pay my bills, I'll never get a job or place of my own, so why keep trying?" This is irrational and unhealthy as well as self-defeating. We can challenge these types of thoughts, we can tell ourselves something different, "This guy might hire me, I just need to show him that I am a good person to take a chance on. Even if I don't get this job, this interview is good experience for me at my next one. I'm going to get a job sooner or later and then I'll be able to get the things I need". That is challenging our thinking and changing the script in our head so we can focus on more productive thoughts. You can also ask yourself things like, "Do I really know what this guy is going to do?" Challenge your preconceived ideas.

Thought stopping is a hugely important coping skill. We can allow our thoughts to spiral out of control if we are not careful. We can tell ourselves all sorts of irrational things if we aren't paying attention to them. We can pump ourselves up for a conflict just by ruminating about things, telling ourselves we know what is going to happen, or what someone's intentions are when we don't really know any of this. We need to be aware and thought stop. This means you stop the line of thoughts coming into your head and change them. Focus on something completely different. Allow yourself to calm down and once you've done that and can think rationally, revisit the problem and think through it.

The most important thing for you is to find the strategies that work best for you. Meditation is a skill that many people do not want to try. They think it's silly or that it just won't work for them. Maybe, or maybe not, but you won't know until you actually try. Meditation is a pre-anger, pre-trigger coping skill. It is hard to develop habit, but once you do, it can be extremely effective. By learning to meditate, you are teaching yourself to calm down and to slow down. Meditation can help you sleep better and it can help you have better focus. It can lower your blood pressure and it can help relieve anxiety and has many other positive effects on you. By meditating 10-15 minutes per day, you will see positive results in a short amount of time. It is worth the effort it involves.

Mindfulness is also a profoundly important skill. Mindfulness means:

"Focusing awareness by attending body sensation."

-Robert Landry, Ph.D.

Paying attention to what our body is experiencing right now is important.

"Mindfulness requires disciplining the monkey mind and attending to the present in the here and now rather than obsessing about the past or the future."

-Robert Landry, Ph.D.

This means, as a coping skill, we are not worried about what happened or what may happen, we are focused on the present moment, the here and now. To be mindful of your body's sensations as they are happening, and if you are focusing on that, you won't be able to prime yourself or pump yourself up for conflict. To be mindful you need to do a body inventory. Start at your feet and move up through your body, just do a quick check-in. Do this with no value attached to it, no judgments. Just go through and acknowledge how you are feeling, not why you are feeling that way. There are many good books available about mindfulness. Mindfulness is a well-supported practice that has been proven effective through research. The explanations provided here are simplistic in nature; however, to fully understand mindfulness and how it can be beneficial to you, I suggest reading some books on it.

One of the most important things for you to do, is to make sure that your Relapse Prevention plan is specific to your needs. Try different things and find what works for you. Talk to people to get new ideas. Keep an open mind and find new answers.

When creating your Relapse Prevention Plan, add to it places you can go for help. These places may include AA/NA, counseling centers, group therapy, etc. A list of local meeting locations and times can be helpful, also include hotline phone numbers that you can call for help.

There is a really good book that is available for free. It offers many great resources, tips and directions. The book also provides some addresses and phone numbers for re-entry support facilities and is a valuable resource for us. The name of the book is: Roadmap to Reentry, A California Legal guide, 2017 Root & Rebound. You can request a copy by writing to:

Root & Rebound
1730 Franklin Street Ste. 300
Oakland, CA 94612

A well-rounded Relapse Prevention Plan should contain information about a support network, including family, friends, sponsors, etc. Goals are also highly important. What will you be working toward? Goals are plans that we have to invest time and effort into, in order to achieve them. Having and achieving goals will add to our sense of self and to our self-worth and self-esteem. Everything works together to help us live a healthy and productive life. Spend some time with someone you trust that has experience in some of these areas. If you don't have a trusted person, take time to evaluate yourself, your location and your social group, and find out why that is and how you can change it.

CHAPTER TWENTY-TWO: BOARD MISCONCEPTIONS

How often do you hear guys say the Board already knew what they were going to do before the hearing started? What do you think about that? Does that sound professional to you? It does not sound professional to me, and I don't believe it to be true.

Some people will not be granted a date at their current hearing. Recent 115, not likely. Recent confidential, not likely. No self-help classes, not likely. There are some precursors to not being granted a date. Just being incarcerated for a long time and staying out of trouble is not good enough in the eyes of the Board.

Is it possible that the commissioners talk and form an opinion about how ready a person is prior to their hearing? Yes, of course it's possible. If you go to Board with an impressive collection of self-help chronos that address your issues, you have job training and a reasonable amount of time being free of disciplinary problems and have good work reports, then you have a good chance of being found suitable. When we do everything we can to be prepared for our Board hearings and the possibility of our release, we have a chance to get a date.

When I hear people who have received denials say that the board was going to do that no matter what, I am skeptical. What are these guys not telling us? Were they honest with themselves and the Board about their crime? Did they take responsibility? Did they express empathy and insight? Did they express remorse? Could they speak about the groups they have been involved in? Did they have reasonable parole plans? Did they have well-rounded Relapse Prevention Plans? Do some guys get raw deals? Maybe. They may not be able to express themselves in a way that the Board feels is adequate and that is unfortunate. There are guys that are not a threat to the public, but they are unable to express themselves in a way the Board deems adequate.

With that being said, there are also many guys who don't do the work necessary, they don't want to take responsibility or they go into hearings with no humility and they act offended when the Board brings up their past. Really? Your past actions are yours, you have to own them. Why deny the truth? It serves no purpose. Lying and denying only serves to keep you locked up longer. The Board is trained to deal with us, and they get to go home after the hearings are over. Do you think they are affected when someone they feel is not ready stays here?

The Board is doing the job that they are trained to do. Some may feel that they are unfair in hearings, but their job is to err on the side of caution, and keep the public safe. Our job is to prove we are ready to go home, that we have addressed our underlying issues. Remember, we did something pretty horrendous to get a life sentence. When we can recognize how vile our actions were and the depths of destruction we have caused, we are on the right path.

Some guys go into their hearings and think they have full understanding of insight, remorse and empathy and feel that they will be able to express these things to the Board. This can be a problem if they haven't taken the time to talk to someone else who may be able to help them see areas in which they are lacking. People skip this important step for a couple of reasons. One reason is they don't communicate with people who can help them. Another reason, is they can't open up and be honest, because they are afraid of judgment from others. If we can't find people to talk to, how can we be sure that what we are thinking is adequate when we say it. Some things that have to be discussed are difficult. There is shame, guilt, and embarrassment involved and that is hard to overcome. We, as a population, need to create safe places for people to talk about these things without judgment and without gossiping about what we learn. That is our responsibility. Another person's personal information should not be used as a form of currency on the yard. We should not be sharing another person's information so we look better or get acceptance. This is detrimental to our recovery.

Other reasons people get denials is that they are not being honest with us (other inmates) about their crimes. Because of this, they make excuses about why they got a denials and place blame on the board. I actually understand this because prison has a history and culture of judging and ridiculing people that is hard for some to endure. For people to grow, it is important for them to learn to be honest and that is the only way out of here as a lifer.

If you observe and listen to those that say the Board had a decision already made, you will see that most of those guys are still stuck in old habits and ways of thinking. They have excuses for everything, blame others and take short-cuts instead of doing the work necessary. They have not yet learned to be honest with themselves. These are the reasons they get denied. These things all become apparent in an interview with trained professionals that lasts several hours. Think about this, how does a person with all of these defects look to the Board, when the Board also sees people that have actually done the work? Do you think they can recognize the difference? Can you see the difference between those who have and those who have not? The only solution to this is to do the work. It's not easy, it requires hard work and dedication, but it gets so much easier with the more you do. It also becomes more and more rewarding, not just for the board, but for ourselves.

Many of us are lazy quitters and that is a major obstacle to overcome. It can be done though. How often do you think, "Man, I don't want to go to this group today."? That thinking is almost like giving yourself permission not to go. That is the thinking you have to overcome. It's okay to have that thought, but you also must have the commitment to your future to overcome that thought. Don't cut corners. Do the work, remove any reasons the Board has to keep you in prison. The more work you put in, the easier your Board hearing will be.

When you go into your Board hearing and get stuff thrown in your face and you are told how horrible the things that you have done are, and you act surprised or try to defend what you did, what do you think is going to happen? If you're one of the people that thinks the Board has a pre-made decision and they throw this stuff in your face trying to get a response, maybe you're right. However, years of playing the victim will bite you in the behind. When you play the victim, you will attempt to excuse or minimize what you've done, you have given the Board all they need to issue a denial, as they should.

If you have done the work, taken responsibility for your actions and shown insight, you are proving yourself to be suitable. See the difference? Which one do you want to be? Maybe the Board does challenge us in there, that is their job and it is okay. If you've done the work, you will pass the challenge. Don't be the resentful, defensive person in the room. Do the work and grow into a person that represents themself in a mature and responsible way. One that proves you are ready.

Another reason that people may be denied is that they cannot fully talk about their Relapse Prevention Plans. Many people go to Psych Evals and to the Board with shoddy, incomplete plans. They copy them from other people or see something being passed around the yard and copy those. That is not going to cut it. You have to put together plans that are specific to your needs. You have to be able to talk about your plans and answer questions about them. It's not about how pretty they look or how long and complex they are, it is about them being yours. This book includes helpful information on how to build and understand your Relapse Prevention Plans.

If you are unable to speak in depth to the Psych about your plans, it will be obvious to them. It will also be obvious to the Board that you have not done the work. Make your plans about your weaknesses and defects and your strengths, not someone else's. Understand what triggers you and how and why your coping skills work for you.

Don't blame your short-comings on the Board's bias. Do the work. Don't fall into the trap of thinking the Board has already made their decision. Go into your hearing prepared and optimistic. If you get a denial, use it as an opportunity to address everything the Board denied you for and be ready for your next hearing. Again, put in the work. Set goals and work towards them. Goals, goals, goals. Goals are so important, they help us get to where we want to be. You probably didn't have goals when you came to prison. Change that, turn your short-comings into strengths.

Don't substitute your opinion with someone else's. Don't become or continue to be angry and bitter. Let go of that negativity. Set goals and work hard to achieve them and grow into the person you want to be. Find a sponsor and/or a mentor and challenge yourself. Don't blame the Board. Even if your feel like you got a raw deal, put in the work for your next hearing. If you get stuck blaming the Board, you won't be able to do what you need to do to get out. It will become a crutch for you and will be the excuse you need to fail at your next hearing. Overcome that.

We are all "ready" to go home, every single one of us. However, how many of us are actually prepared to go home? There is a big difference in the two. Being prepared means you have done the work necessary to be successful and to pass the tests you will encounter when you re-enter society.

Being prepared means we have put in the work to overcome the character defects, short-comings, and addictions; both thinking and behavioral. It means that we have focused time and energy building our strengths and our qualities. It means we have developed the skills we need to live life on life's terms and to manage our emotions in stressful situations. We have prepared ourselves to cope with life's challenges in a healthy and constructive way. One that does not lead to harming ourselves or others.

Prepare yourself not just for society, but for the Board as well. Be prepared to go into your Board hearing and show that you have put in the work necessary and you are not just "ready" to go home, but you are prepared to go home, to give back to society and to lead a life of quality and integrity.

American Prisoner III

-Still I Rise-

PART THREE

Still I Rise

CHAPTER TWENTY-THREE: STILL I RISE

Part III of <u>American Prison II, Still I Rise</u> is probably the most exciting section of the series, thus far. That's because it's YOUR LIFE; most especially, your life after learning of the teaching and techniques and principles presented herein, and because... it hasn't been written yet.

By applying these principles in our everyday lives, we begin to see and understand that change is possible, that we don't have to remain in the dark caverns of the dungeons of remorse and regret that we've exiled ourselves to by remaining prisoners of time, repeating over and over again yesterday's bad behavior patterns. We can attract what we lacked by utilizing what's inside us all and freeing ourselves of the fear and anger and guilt, finally living up to our potential and tapping into the unseen forces of the Universe where all things are possible, all dreams within our power to fulfill.

Through dedicated work, persistent effort, focused thought, and divinely guided intent, the limitless possibilities that once seemed unattainable arrive at our doorstep as the Universe conspires to provide for our every want and need.

And now it's up to you, your future is in your own hands. It's your choice whether to remain lead-footed and standing on the grave of dreams... or, to RISE UP and leap on the back of the wind to claim the sky and all that is beyond as your own.

Don't allow the courts and the naysayers and the doubters have the final word. If you never give up, you're never defeated.

Still I Rise
(Adapted from the Maya Angelou poem)

You may write me down in history
With your bitter, twisted lies,
You may trod me in the very dirt
But still, like dust, I'll rise.

You may shoot me with your venom,
You may cut me with your eyes,
You may kill me with your hatefulness,
But still, like air, I'll rise.

Do you want to see me broken?
With bowed head and lowered eyes,
Shoulders falling down like teardrops,
Weakened by my soulful cries?

Just like moons and dreams and fireflies,
With the certainty of tides,
Like a torch out of the twilight,
And the morning sun, I rise.

Confined in steel and concrete,
Does it come as a surprise?
Chained, shackled, gagged and blinded,
Forever, Still I Rise.

-adapted by D. Razor Babb

*   *   *

RESOURCES

Prisoner Reentry Network
1201 Martin Luther King, Jr. Way #200
P.O. 71552
Oakland, CA 94612
www.prisonerreentryetwork.org
Promotes successful transition from prison to community. Low cost
solutions to critical problems. Information and assistance.

Paul Brunton Philosophic Foundation Prison Project
4936 NYS Route 414
Burdett, NY 14818
www.paulbrunton.org

Dharma Companions
www.dharmacompanions.wordpress.com
Free nonsectarian books to prisons

Prison Activist Resource Center (PARC)
P.O. 70447, Oakland, CA 94612
Will send you a free prisoner resource directory

PEN Writing Awards for Prisoners
PEN American Center
588 Broadway, Suite 303
New York, NY 10012
https://pen.org/annual-prison-writing-contest

Roadmap to Reentry, A California Legal Guide
Root & Rebound
1730 Franklin Street
Suite 300
Oakland, CA 94612
www.rootandrebound.org/roadmap

California Board of Parole Hearings
P.O. Box 4036
Sacramento, CA 95812

California Lifer Newsletter
P.O. Box 277
Rancho Cordova, CA 95741
https://www.prisonactivist.org/resources/california-lifer-newsletter
Newsletter @ $35 or 100 stamps for prisoners

All of Us or None of Us
1540 Market Street, Suite 490
San Francisco, CA 94102
www.allofusornone.org
Legal services for inmates with children

Coalition for Prisoners' Rights Newsletter
P.O. Box 1911
Santa Fe, NM 87504
http://realcostofprisons.org/
Send self-addressed stamped envelopes for copies of newsletter

The Prison Library Project
c/o *The Claremont Forum*
915-C W. Foothill Blvd, PMB 128
Claremont, CA 91711
Free books to prisoners, request by topic

The Prisoners Literature Project
c/o The Grassroots House Collective
2022 Blake Street
Berkeley, CA 94704
www.prisonersliteratureproject.com
Free books to prisoners, request by topic

Alcoholics Anonymous
General Service Office, ATTN: Corrections Desk
475 Riverside Drive
11th Floor
New York, NY 19115
Outside support and pre-release program, among other resources

Prisoners' Guerrilla Handbook to Correspondence Programs in the United States and Canada: High School, Vocational, Paralegal and College Courses by Jon Marc Taylor
Biddle Publishing Co.
13 Gurnet Road, PMB 103,
Brunswick, ME 04011
Provides contact information and an outline of the courses offered by over 250 educational providers, including many major universities. The book includes information on high school, vocational, paralegal, law, college and graduate courses. The book has many useful tips and articles for the proactive prisoner, including how to acquire a college degree for less than $2,000. Cost is $25.95 (postage prepaid) to prisoners.

BIBLIOGRAPHY

Paul Brunton – <u>Perspectives, The Timeless Way of Wisdom</u>
<u>Meditations for Crisis Management</u>

Dr. Wayne Dyer – <u>The Power of Intention</u>
<u>Pulling Your Own Strings</u>

Dr. David Hawkins – <u>Power vs. Force, The Hidden Determinants of</u>
<u>Human Behavior</u>

Rhonda Byrne – <u>The Secret</u>

Napoleon Hill – <u>Think and Grow Rich</u>

Joseph Murphy – <u>The Miracle Power of Your Mind</u>

Leah Ward-Lee - <u>$1,000 Start-Ups</u>

Marci Shimoff – <u>Chicken Soup for the Mother's Soul</u>

Denis Waitley, PhD – <u>The Psychology of Winning</u>

Charles Haanel – <u>The Master Key System</u>

Robert Collier – <u>The Secret of the Ages</u>

Jonathan Haidt – <u>The Happiness Hypothesis</u>

Paramahansa Yogananda – <u>Autobiography of a Yogi</u>

Carlos Castaneda – <u>The Active Side of Infinity</u>
<u>The Fire From Within</u>

David Bohm – <u>Wholeness and the Implicate Order</u>

Lynne McTaggart – The Field: The Quest for the Secret Force of the Universe

Dr. Robert Landry – The 2 x 2 Anger Response Model

D. Razor Babb – American Prisoner I, Above the Cage, a prisoner's personal self-help and rehabilitation guide

Gerry Spense – How to Argue and Win Every Time

Heidi Yewman – Beyond the Bullet

Beverly Engel – Honor Your Anger

Matthew Mckay, PhD, Peter Rogers, PhD – The Anger Control Workbook

Carl Semmelroth, PhD – The Anger Habit Workbook

Susan Forward, PhD, Donna Frazier – Emotional Blackmail

Hazeldon Books – Socialization
Criminal Addictive Thinking
Relapse Prevention

Howard Zehr – Transcending: Reflection of Crime Victims

Barb Toews – Restorative Justice for People in Prison

Viktor E. Frankel – Man's Search for Meaning

Alexander L. Chapman, PhD, Kim L. Gratz, PhD – The DBT Skills Workbook for Anger

Jim Catheart – The Acorn Principle

Joseph V. Bailey – The Serenity Principle

ABOUT THE AUTHORS

D. RAZOR BABB

After a 60-foot fall during an attempted escape, D. Razor Babb soon discovered that true freedom and fulfillment would only be found through serious introspection, sincere self-evaluation, and a pen and paper

D. Razor Babb is a former reporter, PEN Writing Awards winner and founding editor of the *Corcoran Sun and Mule Creek Post,* prison yard papers. After writing and publishing five novels that spanned the detective noir and dystopian genres he began to focus his writing on books that would inspire and assist other prisoners to find a purpose and learn to believe there was the potential for a future.

THOMAS J. DUNAWAY

Thomas is a juvenile lifer who has spent 24 years in prison and has dedicated his life to helping others change theirs. He spends his time educating himself so that he can share what he learns with others in the hope of making his community a better place, with the goal of stopping the victimization of others. He is working on becoming a Substance Abuse Counselor.

OTHER BOOKS BY D. RAZOR BABB & FROM THE PUBLISHER

AMERICAN PRISONER I, Above the Cage: A prisoner's personal self-help and rehabiliation guide. Are you ready to go home? More lifers, juvenile offenders and elderly inmates will be going before parole board in the coming monhs than ever before. AMERICAN PRISONER gets you ready for board and a whole new life. The ability to tap into your own unlimited potential and achieve your highest dreams is not only possible, it's at your fingertips and waiting for you to discover. Over 20 years of exhaustive study, research and real life application has led to this comprehensive personal guide that any person can follow to gain control of his or her own higher power. No one is going to help you unless you help yourself; take control of your life and start living today. 154 pages. $14.99

BABB'S WRITER'S WORKSHOP: How to Write & Publish from Inside. Learn how to write and publish novels, memoirs, essays, short stories, articles and autobiographies from someone who started fom nothing and has done it from inside. Everybody's got a story, what's yours? This workbook takes you from idea to page in easy to understand steps, and shows you how to access that untapped, unlimited creativity that the most famous authors are familiar with. Interesting characters and story plots are all around you, learn how to take the seemingly mundane and turn it into something wonderful. The greatest stories ever written were once nothing more than an idea. Your ideas are just as valid as any others, just as interesting. Learn how to harness that raw talent and create something of value. 120 pgs, 9x12" workbook. $9.99

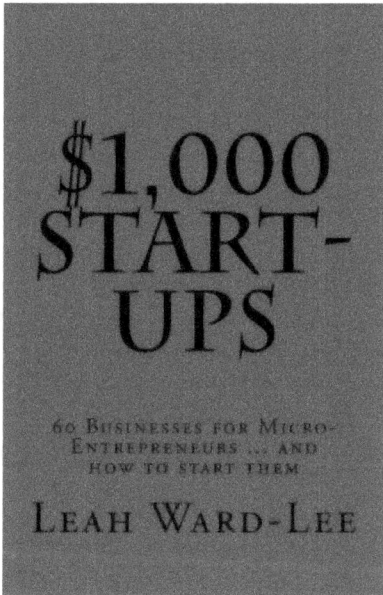

$1,000 START-UPS: Sixty businesses for Micro-Entrepreneurs and How to Start Them. Owning a business is the deal changer that puts you in control of your destiny If you want to get started as an entrepreneur this book tells you how and provides all the tools you need to get started for less than $1,000. This author is a successful serial entrepreneur and business consultant who has learned through experience and trial & error the best avenues to follow to be a successful entrepreneur. If you're ready to be in control of your financial future $1,000 START-UPS may be just what you need to make the move from concept to business including a full-blown business plan, record keeping, marketing and managerment. 521 pgs. $24.99

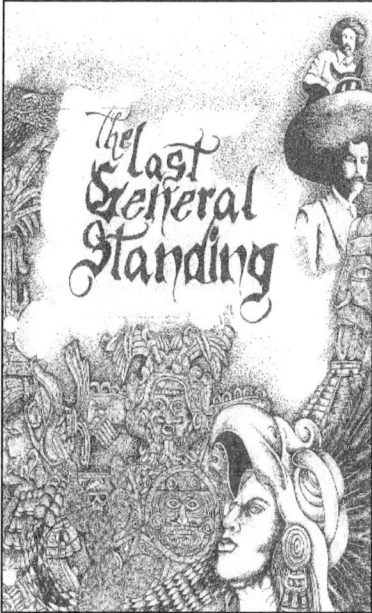

THE LAST GENERAL STANDING by J. Figueroa: This is the true story of a kid who went to prison for stealing a car, killed another inmate during a gang war, then ended up doing time for the 'Nuestra Familia', one of the most notorious prison Gangs in California.

"Give me your word my Brother, and betray me no more,
If you need my help, here I am waiting,
Waiting day after day, for your hand I'll be waiting."

From: "The Song of the Nuestra Familia" $14.99

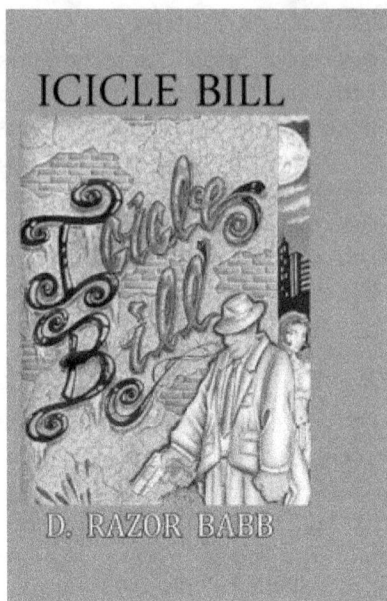

ICICLE BILL: The original action-adventure classic that started it all. A car-jacking in L.A. forces a guy who is barely able to cope with his own problems into a whirlwind of conflict and adventure involving a bizarre cast of characters straight out of a Tarantino movie. From Los Angeles high rises to the bleached desert sands of Vulture Flats, Icicle Bill and his sidekick Tommy Two-Head dodge bullets, the authorities and their own tortured pasts in an effort to save the beautiful sister of a Mexican gangbanger and struggle to witness just one more sunrise. Intrigue and danger stalks them all the way to Vegas, as quiet & ominous as blood drops on sand. 223 pgs. $14.95

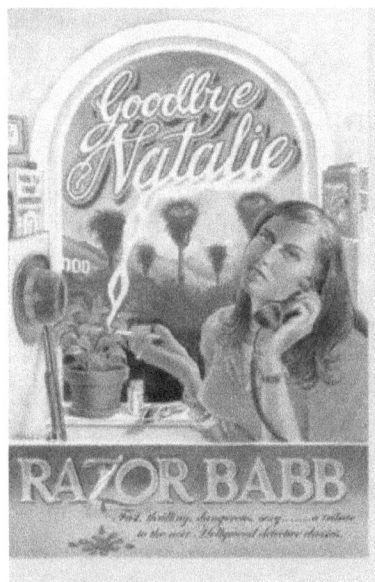

GOODBYE NATALIE: The first Fallon Dawn Hunter, girl detective book in the series, Kansas farmgirl Fallon Hunter lands in Hollywood and quickly discovers that not everyone who is nice to you is your friend. She lands a temp job in a ramshackle Hollywood detective agency and when the owner turns up dead, embarks on her own investigation to find out what happened. Along the way she meets a famous Hollywood film legend, is introduced to the seedy underworld of sex traffickers, and finds herself the target of a ruthless killer. She's traded in snow boots for stilettos and her little dog for a Colt .25, only to discover you can't run from killers in heels and you can't always stop what's chasing you with bullets. 315 pgs. $14.95

144

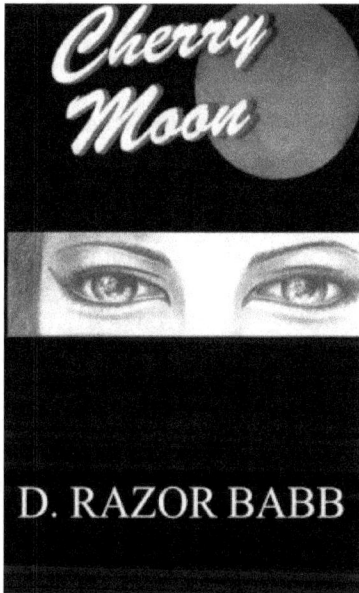

CHERRY MOON: The second book in the Fallon Dawn Hunter, girl detective series. Fallon Hunter has taken over A-1 Detective Agency in Hollywood and becomes involved in an investigation that is way over her head. For a brief period in the 1980's the skies over L.A. were illuminated by a mysterious red glow that the local media dubbed, CHERRY MOON. Many theories were presented but none explained the anomaly. Some saw it as a lucky omen, others would disagree. When Fallon is hired to find a missing girl, who was last seen in the company of a dead man, she soon learns there are no simple cases and she may have bitten off more than she can swallow. A tribute to the detective noir classics, R-rated. 520 pgs. $17.99

OUTCAST: In the future, mankind is at the brink of annihilation and forced to live in domed communities. At birth, infants are implanted with microchip technology called sliders that feed all the knowledge, data and resources needed for a lifetime directly to their brain via S.O.U.R.C.E. Criminal or deviant behavior is punishable by banishment to the outland, one strike and you're OUTCAST. In the outland chances at survival are nil, underground tunnels are inhabited by mutants and predators and topside radiation is a death sentence. Cut off from S.O.U.R.C.E. without even a memory of who you are or were or where you came from, there is no less hopeless fate than to be OUTCAST. 321 pgs. $14.99

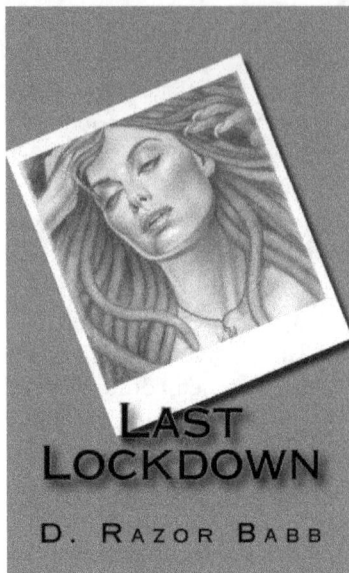

LAST LOCKDOWN: The End of the World is only the beginning of the Story ....

"We knew things were bad, but we didn't know how bad. When the electricity went off, we figured it wouldn't be for long. Prison is a separate reality from the outside – we're largely detached from what goes on out there. So at first we thought the problems, whatever they were, wouldn't affect us much, we were wrong. That first day they came around and tossed bag lunches into the cells; all the guards were ashen-faced and wouldn't tell us anything. The radio and TV stations were off the air; battery-powered radios and TV's got nothing but static. The next day nobody showed up for work – no guards, medical staff, maintenance – nobody. By the third day we realized if we were going to survive, it was on us." 270 pgs. $14.99

www.ingramcontent.com/pod-product-compliance
Lightning Source LLC
La Vergne TN
LVHW052028080426
835513LV00018B/2213